Collabor

Collaborative Stewardship:

Analytical Approach for Improving Quality of Life in Communities

Collaborative Stewardship: An Analytical Approach to Improving Quality of Life in Communities

Authored by Olivia M. McDonald, Ph.D.

Printed in the United States of America

Library of Congress Cataloguing in Publication Data.

ISBN-13: 978-0- 9835652-4- 6 *Collaborative Stewardship* E-book

ISBN-13: 978-0- 9835652-7- 7 *Collaborative Stewardship* Paperback

ISBN-13: 978-0-9835652-8-4 *Collaborative Stewardship* Hardback

1. Collaborative Stewardship. 2. Community Economic Development. 3. Collaborative Monitoring. 4. Evaluative Measures. 5. Social Network Analysis for Evaluation

I. McDonald, Olivia M. 1954 -

Cover Art Work: Painting by Charles Angrand, 1887

Collaborative Stewardship

TO THOSE CALLED
TO REDEEM THE LAND

Collaborative Stewardship

CONTENTS

LIST OF TABLES AND FIGURES

PREFACE

Collaborative Stewardship: Analytical Approach to Improving Quality of Life in Communities rests upon the idea that community should be seen as a living organism, one for which specific functions need to be in working order for the community to survive and then operate at peak performance. To date, researchers have tended to approach development from the perspective of community actors and actions rather than assessing the overall vitality of the jurisdiction, which if the answer to that question were pursued, it would entail giving consideration to the systematic review of contagion and interdependency of internal workings associated with the configuration of entities resident there.

Consider this analogy: Imagine a patient visiting a doctor because of a pain in the patient's foot. When asked what happened, the patient explains that the pain began after tripping over something at home two weeks ago; and, the pain is getting worse every day. If the doctor simply hands the patient a prescription for pain relief and does nothing else, then the visit missed the mark. *Why?* Because questions need to be answered, questions like:

-Why has the pain persisted so long over what was described as a simple misstep?

-Why is the pain increasing in severity?

-What factors may be at work within the body to render this discomfort?

-And, what is going wrong in the body that may have rendered susceptibility to falling?

Just as when medical personnel effectively facilitate health and healing of the human body by pursuing remedies that maximize the likelihood that the bodily functions associated with internal organs (units of organization) work together to promote health, so must we examine community in terms of the functional elements required for its vitality.

What strategies deserve consideration when attempting to evaluate the efforts of multiple stakeholders and the entities they represent in the service of communities? That is the question this text has been designed to address. I posit that such evaluations must be conducted; and, that those activities must be approached as a sacred trust of stewardship. Said activities can be examined mechanistically stressing the relation between goals and functions performed.

Introduced here are 1) a paradigm for evaluating collaborative policy and program activity; and, 2) parameters within which such evaluations may take place.

Some researchers focus on organizations, what organizations interact with other organizations, often producing elaborate accounts of attributes, relative connectivity, and sometimes solvency. However, such conversation tends to remain merely descriptive of interaction devoid of concern for purpose; and, more importantly, those discussions omit concern for collective impact of combined interactions on outcomes for the quality of life for the community.

Having said that, please note that I am not saying that the pattern of interaction should be discarded from further exploration. Rather, what is argued here is that detection of pattern of exchange is only a first step. Inquiry remains incomplete until outcome is linked to pattern of functional interaction. And, by function, I am speaking of both internal and external deliverables that contribute to community well-being. Also, of concern is the nature and scope of the rendering of such functions to determine whether the activity is sufficient for the task at hand. It is only then that an effective assessment of functions performed by the entities involved can be tweaked for purposes of improving quality of life within a community. Further, in documenting the nature of configurative response to challenges within a community, it is possible to isolate best practices in context,[1] identifying most similar and most different systems of operation along with the outcomes produced. Level of analysis may then be elevated from simple display of isolated social network graphics and the challenges normally associated with those metrics, to one of a higher posture of analysis, that of detecting the consequences of connections, thus identifying patterns for purposes of testing the relationship between the presence of certain patterns and the resulting outcomes. And, then with evidence-based research, we are in a better position to determine the best sequence of configurative interactions in support of the vital functions of the community.

Once the desired goals are specified, monitoring and evaluation can take place. Indeed, quality control indicators may be put in place which would be useful not only for monitoring normal operations (having established thresholds of acceptability) for the community; but,

[1] See Adam Przeworski and Henry Teune. *The Logic of Comparative Social Inquiry*. New York: Wiley-Interscience, 1970

this may prove useful also for detecting anomalies indicative of man-made adversity.

With such a thorough understanding the status of the community/jurisdiction, collaborative stewards will be in a better position to not only respond but to return to normalcy the operations required for the jurisdiction in the event of a disaster.

Collaborative Stewardship: Analytical Approach to Improving Quality of Life in Communities presents tools that would be useful for considering what should be done to improve communities.

This text consists of three parts:

Part 1 - *Accountability*. Part 2 - *Discrepancy*. Part 3 - *Change*.

The operative theme of this work is stewardship. What differentiates this work from other materials is the focus on analytical tools to the benefit of communities who wish to pursue collaborative stewardship. Methods discussed may be employed to maximize accountability among collaborative entities, identifying discrepancies between what is required and what is actually observed in the execution of responsibilities to and among citizens of a community. The analytical approach recommended here is one that tracks the performance of functions for the purpose of improving quality of life in communities.

This is a Biblically-informed work.

To God be the glory, *Amen!*

Olivia McDonald, 2016

COLLABORATIVE STEWARDSHIP PROMOTES THE
FAITHFUL MONITORING OF
ACCOUNTABILITY, DISCREPANCY, AND CHANGE
FOR THE IMPROVEMENT OF QUALITY OF LIFE IN COMMUNITIES.

----*OLIVIA M. MCDONALD, PH.D.*

Collaborative Stewardship

PART ONE: ACCOUNTABILITY

1

COLLABORATIVE LINKS AS A LEVEL OF ANALYSIS PROBLEM

"Can two walk together unless they are agreed?"
Amos 3:3, *Holy Bible* (NKJV)

Collaborative Stewardship Defined. Collaborative Stewardship by Whom? Why Collaborative Stewardship should be undertaken. How performed? Assessing Effectiveness. Creating Collaborative Stewardship Action Statements. Recognizing Collaborative Points. What Can Go Wrong? How to Avoid Pitfalls.

What is meant by collaborative stewardship?

By collaborative stewardship I am referring to the efforts made by individual organizations to work in a coordinated fashion for the accomplishment of a shared vision that promotes life within a community. By collaborative stewardship I am not referring to commissions, more conferences, nor simply joint projects; but rather, to concerted activity associated with a number of stages beginning with the development of a shared vision of community that yields concrete milestones established with clearly specified outcomes in mind. Progress toward the accomplishment of well-defined goals then becomes detectable as a consequence of careful monitoring of quality of life in the jurisdiction.

In essence, I am referring to a God-ordained guardianship that is accountable to the community. Again, such a responsibility requires the monitoring if very specific indicators, measures seen in relation to explicit goals, both formative (process-oriented) and summative (overall impact oriented,) work in the form of sustained attention to detail in order to prevent adversity and to correct where necessary the functions that falls short of the collective –life promoting--vision of community.

To whom does the exercise of collaborative stewardship refer?

Collaborative stewardship pertains to the full assortment of stakeholders who provide services within a jurisdiction. Those stakeholders would include but not be limited to governmental entities and non-governmental entities: community-based organizations, non-profit organizations, private organizations, businesses, educational institutions, medical institutions, public service entities, and religious organizations. In other words, the collaborative stewardship constitutes vigilant pursuit of the betterment of the community via collective action.

How is collaborative stewardship to be performed?

Collaborative stewardship will be performed through monitoring of accountability, discrepancy, and change in the community that may be facilitated by the configuration of entities within a geographic area.

Again, the key terms are:

Accountability

Discrepancy

Change

Collaborative stewardship occurs in three overlapping stages. The first consists of the establishment of accountability for the collective impact of efforts performed within the jurisdiction This entails not only identifying all of the actors for specific jurisdiction but also identifying or otherwise securing a detailed account the functions performed and to what consequence. It also means identifying the obstacles to optimal performance. And it involves the implications associated with performance deficiencies within the organization, recognizing that the impact those deficiencies may have as a rippling effect throughout the full tapestry of organizations serving a geographical area.

Once identified the organizations need to recognize not only the operative status of their individual organization but also the consequences of their operations on other organizations; and, ultimately on the quality of life for the entire community.

It is not sufficient for organizations to know their status and the status of other organizations without tangible commitment to a strategic plan or shared vision of the direction in which the community is to move. That also means identifying the challenges confronting the community, meaning the scope and severity a problem the community may be experiencing. It also means the identification of pockets of sub-populations that may be more vulnerable to the challenges confronting the community.

Once this information is garnered, the next step is to determine the degree to which coverage of challenges is taking place by the current configuration of service providing entities. There is a need to discover whether the system of operations within a location are compatible to the actual needs of that jurisdiction. A determination is to be made as to the implications about the configurative pattern. Are there any disparities in access to needed elements? Do the resources garnered by entities that make up the configuration actually translate into improved life for the community at-large and do so equitably, not omitting sub-populations that experience the severe need.

Such information may prove to be a very useful instrument for individuals who wish to evaluate the cost-effectiveness of resource allocation for a specific jurisdiction. In addition, this approach will uncover discrepancies in planned vs. observed activity and/or execution of programs and policies is currently in place in the location.

Recommendations can then be made as to what would constitute appropriate configuration of activity and allocation of resources for the community.

The above reflects impact analysis. The procedure for reaching this point of analysis will require process evaluation.

The steps to be accomplished for collaborative stewardship will be discussed in detail in this book.

Why should collaborative stewardship be undertaken?

Collaborative stewardship should be undertaken because organizations that purport to serve the public should do so with accountability to the public. Such organizations should not simply pursue daily activities in a vacuum but responsibly to the community

Recent events in Flint Michigan serve as a reminder that accountability is not guaranteed but requires vigilance.

Further, given the expense that is associated with potential waste from poor decision-making, collaborative stewardship is a way of preventing needless challenges to a community. Stewardship requires monitoring the activities the best interest of the residents of the community.

All the literature speaks of the importance of political involvement with such operations encompassing what is referred to as deliberative policy involving the population. Such efforts do not guarantee that operations will be in the best interest of those who live in the jurisdiction.

What I am proposing here will permit the evaluation of best practices and provide a platform for evidence-based research useful to inform the direction taken by locations that once encountered comparable problems, perhaps due to mal-aligned configurative structures and/or resource levels.

How will you know when collaborative stewardship operations have been effectively implemented?

Collaborative stewardship is effective if the following occurs:

Organizations conduct in managerial audit of their internal operations which includes an assessment at each level of organization concerning what the perceived goals and objectives are of the organization at-large and the specific units within the organization. Related will be the perspective as to how the individual parts within the organization contribute to the mission at-large.

Organizations review the stated officially mandated goals and objectives originating with the founders of the entity, or in the case of governmental operations, the legislative and regulatory mandates.

The review serves as the point of departure between stated and/or mandated goals and to the actual perceived goals within the organization. Once detected, deficiencies can be addressed. Future reviews are then to be conducted to determine if a change in mission is warranted or if there needs to be an internal readjustment of operation.

A review is made of the decided upon or otherwise mandated goals and objectives of entities across the jurisdiction in order to determine the landscape of entities that are working to achieve similar goals. This will allow for the determination of whether there exists necessary or unnecessary redundancy with regard to operations and the allocation unlimited resources.

Organizations will be able to identify specific functions they perform for the betterment of the community and to what degree it would the prudent to establish partnerships in those efforts. It may be discovered that an organization may be better equipped to work on different functions that is to say a reallocation of effort such that one organization does function a, b, and c and another organization does function d and f, all of which are required for the accomplishment of the originally stated goal. This may lead to greater efficiency and effectiveness again in the service of the community. It also may prove to be useful for the minimization of waste and the misallocation of effort for the jurisdiction.

A comparison can be made between what exists in terms of service provision for a jurisdiction and what is required because collaborative stewardship allows for the collective review of operations that impact the community. The evaluation becomes one of existing functional positioning of organizations compared to what would be the more appropriate configuration given the internal dynamics of the community and best practices uncovered via evidence-based research.

These evaluation efforts will allow for the development of most appropriate recommendations for change for the betterment of the community. And, individual organizations will benefit because there will be a true assessment of the relative contribution each of the organizations actually makes to quality of life.

When these things occur, collaborative stewardship will be in effect.

What can go wrong?

Challenges can occur within a community for which there is such a political backlash that organizations will be reluctant to partner or share information with other organizations and the public in the jurisdiction.

Periods of increased competitiveness for extremely limited resources may prove to be an obstacle to efforts for collaboration as each organization pursues survival as over favorable collective impact as the primary goal.

Also, some organizations may perceive themselves as having intellectual property that they may not wish for others to view especially if that intellectual property is directly related to the way they function and has gleaned success beyond the efforts of other organizations in the area.

And, with regard to government entities, all of the typical challenges that have been well-documented and public policy literature apply. These may prove a hindrance to the adaptation of collaborative stewardship in governance. [2]

Nevertheless, given all of the objections, collaborative stewardship if executed even in only a few sectors of a jurisdiction should render greater impact for the betterment of those sections and that community than if there were no move in that direction. Hence it is worth the effort to attempt this strategy.

---

[2] See Paul A. Sabatier, *Theories of the Policy Process*. Boulder, Colorado: Westview Press, 2007. Also see: Richard E. Matland(1995) "Synthesizing the Implementation Literature: The Ambiguity-Conflict Model of Policy Implementation." *Journal of Public Administration Research and Theory*. J-PART, 5, no. 2. 145-174.

Worksheet for Applying Figure 1.1

Specify the following for a selected problem area associated with your jurisdiction.:

Problem or Desired Outcome (Y):

Theories (Explanation associated with Y) with full citations where appropriate (X_i):

Goals/Objectives ($Y_{i+\ldots+}Y_n$):

Sub-Objectives ($S_{i+\ldots+}S_n$):

Combined Functions (x_i):

Functions Between Organizations ($f_{i.t}$):

Functions Within Organizations: ($f_{i.a.i}$)

Figure 1.1 Hierarchal Equations Based on Configuration Functions Contextual Adding

Theories (Explanations) for Y: $Y = X_1 + X_2 + \ldots + X_n$

Goals and Objectives: $Y_1 = x_{1.1} + x_{1.2} + \ldots + x_{1.n}$

Sub-Objectives: $X_{1.1} = S_{1.1} + S_{1.2} + \ldots + S_{1.n}$

Combined Functions: $x_1 = f_{1.1} + f_{1.2} + \ldots + f_{1.n}$

Functions Between Organizations: $f_{1.1} = t_{1.1} + t_{1.2} + \ldots + t_{1.n}$

Functions Within Organizations: $f_{1.11} = a_{1.1} + a_{1.2} + \ldots + a_{1.n}$
Levels(units)/Dimensions

Where, Y = Goal (Either to secure that which is of value or minimize the adverse impact.)

X = Explanation for Y
x = Objectives that must be achieved to yield Y
T or t = Treatment
f = Function(s) to be performed given the explanation
a = activities/tasks

Weights should be assigned on the basis of relative importance to goal achievement.

How do you avoid pitfalls?

The best starting place for the execution of collaborative stewardship as a strategy for your jurisdiction will be in prayer. God can grant favor for such activity and will grant wisdom to those who ask for it. Prayer should go before planning. Prayer should be the first step for the communication with others in order to know how and when to best present the idea. Prayer should be instrumental in the development and formation of criteria for assessing the needs of the community.

Because decision-making often is a problem solving issue and not necessarily one of maximizing utilities, a series of tools exist in the form of research methodology that will allow one to understand the nature of the questions that may be answered in addressing the challenges confronting the community, granting the ability to identify the scope and severity of those challenges in conjunction with information on the amount of change that has occurred as a consequence of organizational response.

What analytical framework should we pursue?

An organizational network-wide view, that which is discussed here, points to questions concerning planned versus observed linkages between functional entities (with functions performed within and between organizations), all of which are required to work collaboratively in the achievement of specified goals. Such a network wide view may answer the following questions:

- What would be optimal?
- What should be the tolerated minimum operationally?
- Do aspects of the configuration adversely bring about selective destruction of benefit and/or decline in the community?
- What is the impact of the topology or sequence of output from these

organizations?

Finally, the summative question, that which is associated with change is:

- What difference does the configurative pattern of intervention make?

Thus, monitoring the degree to which,

Configuration[3] → Outcome

With improvement of conditions contingent upon conditions interacting with configurative response.

Comparative Configuration Impacts

Review of findings, evidence-based research through the systematic examination of documented outcomes provides the ability to explore the configuration impacts experienced under comparable conditions in a variety of jurisdictions, examining not only the scope and severity covered but also the potential transferability of strategy employed in keeping with change in configurative platforms.

Structural Imagery:

Stinchcombe (1987) identifies the basic attributes of structural imagery, components of which include tension and homeostasis interacting to produce and/or maintain structure.[4] Embedded in this imagery is the mechanism for demand absorption. One can speak of system tension in quantitative terms. The advantage of using such

[3] Although the point of emphasis is on organizational configuration, the level of individual initiative characteristic of the geographical area must be taken into consideration as a critical component for successful stewardship.
[4] See Arthur L. Stinchcombe. *Constructing Social Theories*. Chicago: University of Chicago Press. 1987.

imagery is that one can picture the potential outcome seen as the result of dynamic interaction among major entities. In *Acknowledging God in the Decisions of State*, I posit that there is a problem redefinition process that takes place as a result of individual citizen frequency of engagement with an entity, especially public sector, and even more so if that encounter is regulatory or one of dependency.[5] The notion of equilibrium enabled by tension absorption due to the structural dynamics at work is well understood in the social sciences.[6]

Collaborative Stewardship demands concern for outcomes, tangible indicators of quality of life experienced within a jurisdiction. Conceptual and operational definitions of indicators to be monitored must be clearly specified and linked to goals, objectives, sub-objectives, functions performed within and between entities in response to conditions.

---

[5]McDonald, Olivia M. *Acknowledging God in the Decisions of State: A Treatise on Biblically-Informed Statesmanship.* 2nd Ed. Suffolk, VA: Grace House Publishing, 2015.

[6] See *When Formality Works: Authority and Abstraction in Law and Organization* by Arthur L. Stinchcombe. Chicago: University of Chicago Press. 2001.

Figure 1.2 – Functional Configuration of Network Parts and Sub-Parts

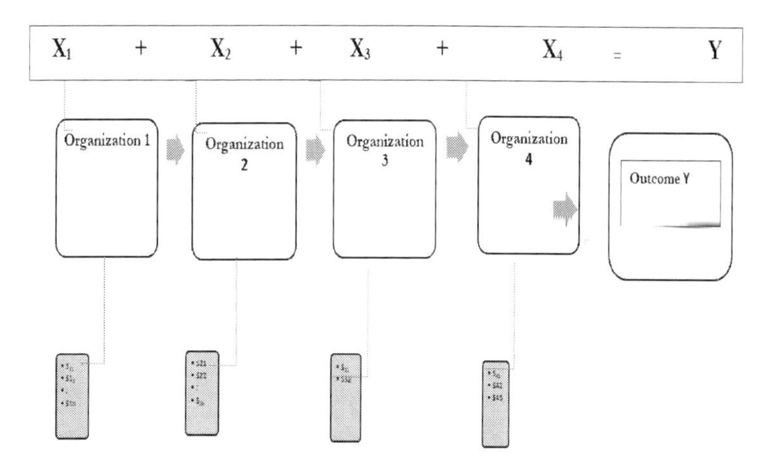

Common research methods associated with applied research endeavors may prove useful for monitoring change in network configuration. For example,

Trend Analysis answers the question, *"If we continue along the same path as a collective configuration of functions served, what will be the outcome?"*

Simulation/Sense-Making can help answer the question, *"What scenarios may result from the current level or mode of operation?"*

Risk Assessment/Optimization can address the question, *"What limits the possibility of change in outcome?"*

Interrupted Time Series Analysis: *"With the intervention at a given point of time, what change in outcome may be detected?"*

Impact Analysis: *"What difference did the intervention make?"*

Consider Where Social Network Analysis (SNA) May Prove Useful:

With additional nodes so that relations cease to be depicted as static, SNA[7] may prove useful in answering both first- and second-order evaluative questions. The first order questions consist of questions that address the formative aspects of network operations for which there may be fluctuation in perceived nature of relations that have consequence for operations. The key elements are first presented by Hidalgo-Hardeman (1993).[8]

They include:

- Diversity of objectives
- Functional design/objectives
- Diversity of subpart functions
- Funding source dependency
- Expenditure/priority

---

[7] For an understanding of Social Network Analysis methodology, see: Ronald S. Burt and Michael J. Minor. *Applied Network Analysis: A Methodological Introduction*. Beverly Hills: Sage Publications, 1983. Also see: Stanley Wasserman and Joseph Galaskiewicz(eds.) 1994. *Advances in Social Network Analysis*. Thousand Oaks: Sage Publications.

[8] Olivia M. Hidalgo-Hardeman. 1993. "Evaluating Social Service Delivery Configurations." *Evaluation Review*. 17, no. 6: 603-20.

- Insulation
- Network-wide decision points
- Budget allocation/network-wide financial distribution
- Rates of dissolution of network subparts/functions
- Concentration of service type
- Number of network subpart functions
- Number (rate) of additions to subpart functions
- Number (rate) of subpart consolidations
- Point of union of diverse/similar subparts
- Plan development actors
- Timeframe of resource life
- Reputational scores
- Concentration of actors influential in the subpart activity

To the extent that operations are multichannel, the evaluations require determining whether the initiative and its outcome exist as consequence of pre-existing structure/functional characteristics updating of cognitive maps, the typical research plan ingredients derived from an understanding of Yin (2003) would include the following:

- Identification of principle actors and administrative responsibility
- Determination of the objectives of each operation and the extent of overlap
- Determination of the degree to which legislative or executive mandate is stifled or facilitated by the administrative arrangement
- Comparison across time changes in the major program requirements
- Comparison across time changes in program administrative outputs
- Comparison across time changes in targeting requirements[9]

What the Nelson-Matthews Cause Map[10] strategy would add to inquiry at this juncture includes the measure of complexity based upon the perspective of stakeholders. The elements that would include are consistent with prevailing notions of complexity involve:

- The number of variables that affect a subunit
- The number of subunits that apply inputs in the form of workflows into a given unit
- The number of interactions between variables and subunits that impact a given subunit

[9] See Robert K. Yin, *Case Study Research: Design and Methods*. Thousand Oaks: Sage Publications. 2003. Also see, Robert K. Yin *Applications of Case Study Research*. Thousand Oaks: Sage Publications. 2003.

[10] See Reed E. Nelson and K. Michael Mathews, "Cause Maps and Social Network Analysis in Organizational Diagnosis," *Journal of Applied Behavioral Science*. September 1991 vol. 27 no. 3 379-397.

- The number of variables or subunits in which a given subunit shares causality

Chapter 1 – A Closing Note

Our principal collaborator must be God. We must operate in a way that is consistent with His written word, the Holy Bible. We may then move forward by first creating accurate assessments of the problems confronting a community. Problem definition is critical to this process as misspecification can undermine our efforts. Then, we must prayerfully seek guidance from God for affiliations with whom collaboration will yield good result. Do understand this: Accountability to God and then to man will help us avoid error associated with problem misspecification, that which would otherwise later pose additional challenges in implementation and outcome.[11] *As this text unfolds, we will discuss those subsequent elements in greater detail. But for now, let's simply take an analytical snapshot of your community. Complete Exercise 1. Inventory of Organizations.*

EXERCISE 1 - INVENTORY OF ORGANIZATIONS

1.1 Take an inventory of organizations operative in your jurisdiction.

1.2 On the basis of the information gleaned, select or otherwise derive a configuration of need based upon documented scope and severity of problem(s) confronting the community.

1.3 Map geographically the density of problematic elements confronting the jurisdiction.

---

[11] See McDonald, Olivia M. McDonald, *Acknowledging God in the Decisions of State: A Treatise on Biblically-Informed Statesmanship.* 2nd Ed. Suffolk, VA: Grace House Publishing, 2015.

1.4 Identify the organizations perceived to have been designated to respond to aspects of the stated problem(s).

1.5 Determine the obstacles to addressing the specific problem(s).

1.6 Identify status and reported frequency response to the score and severity of the problem.

1.7 Pinpoint the actors within the configuration that share responsibility for addressing the problem.

1.8 Report findings.

SUGGESTED READING

Accountability

Rist, Ray C. (1989), "Management Accountability: The Signals Sent by Auditing and Evaluation", *Journal of Public Policy*, 9 (3), July/September, 355-69.

Configuration

Eisenberg M, and N Swanson. 1996. "Organizational Network Analysis as a Tool for Program Evaluation." *Evaluation & the Health Professions.* 19, no. 4: 488-506.

Molina, Jose Luis. 2001. "The Informal Organizational Chart in Organizations: An Approach from the Social Network Analysis." *Connections*, 24(1): 78-91.

Müller-Prothmann, Tobias. *Leveraging Knowledge Communication for Innovation Framework, Methods, and Applications of Social Network Analysis in Research and Development.* Frankfurt am Main: Peter Lang, 2006.<http://public.eblib.com/choice/publicfullrecord.aspx?p=1056265>.

Saaty, Thomas L. and Luis G. Vargas. Decision *Making in Economic, Politic, Social and Technological Environments with the Analytic Hierarchy Process.* Pittsburgh: RWS Publications.1994.

Mapping Problem

Effectiveness. Thousand Oaks, Calif: Sage, 2005.
<http://public.eblib.com/choice/publicfullrecord.aspx?p=3032344>.

Chen, Huey-tsyh. *Theory-Driven Evaluations*. Newbury Park, Calif: Sage Publications, 1990.

Chen, Huey-tsyh, and Peter H. Rossi. *Using Theory to Improve Program and Policy Evaluations*. New York: Greenwood Press, 1992.

Schoen MW, S Moreland-Russell, K Prewitt, and BJ Carothers. 2014. "Social Network Analysis of Public Health Programs to Measure Partnership". *Social Science & Medicine (1982)*. 125: 90-5

Obstacles

Durand, Roger, Phillip J. Decker, and Dorothy M. Kirkman. 2014. "Evaluation Methodologies for Estimating the Likelihood of Program Implementation Failure." *American Journal of Evaluation*. 35, no. 3: 404-418.

Response

Axelrod, Robert M. *The Structure of Decision: The Cognitive Maps of Political Elites*. 1977.

Shared Responsibility

Gates, E., and L. Dyson. 2016. "Implications of the Changing Conversation About Causality for Evaluators." *American Journal of Evaluation*.

Gill, Jeff. *Bayesian Methods A Social and Behavioral Sciences Approach*. Bayesian Methods. Boca Raton, FL: CRC Press, Taylor & Francis Group, 2015.

McKenny, A.F., Short J.C., and Payne G.T. 2013. "Using Computer-Aided Text Analysis to Elevate Constructs: An Illustration Using Psychological Capital". *Organizational Research Methods*. 16, no. 1: 152-184.

Rogers, Patricia J. 2000. "Causal Models in Program Theory Evaluation". *New Directions for Evaluation*. 2000, no. 87: 47-55.

Rogers, Patricia J. *Program Theory in Evaluation: Challenges and Opportunities*. San Francisco, Calif: Jossey-Bass, 2000.

2

CAUSAL THEORY AND COLLABORATIVE ACTION

"So we rebuilt the wall till all of it reached half of its height, for the
People worked with all of their heart."
–Nehemiah 4:6, *Holy Bible* NIV

-

Lessons Learned from Various Disciplines. Relationship between Theoretical Arguments and Causal Event. Procedural Response Linkages. Resources Juxtaposed to Problem Scope. Requisites. Expectations and Measurement. Working Together to Accomplish What?

Evaluation within the public policy and program cycle has two divisions: Process Evaluation, sometime referred to as formative evaluation, offers an assessment of the mechanistic aspects of the work accomplished. The second, Impact Evaluation, often referred to as summative evaluation, does what the name implies. Impact affords an overall assessment of the difference the intervention made to the society. Process evaluation stresses: (i) a recognized theoretical relation between the desired outcome and the nature of the intervention; (ii) the presence of a program intervention that has an anticipated effect; (iii) the presence of a counterfactual; and, (iv) a recognized method for determining the extent to which the desired effect was realized. See Figure 2.1 for a depiction of problem response.

Causal Theory and Collaborative Activity

Embedded within each stage of process evaluation is implied an intentional structural arrangement that may serve as a point of comparison with that which was actualized. Policy evaluators are well aware that theory-driven approaches to evaluation search diligently for the determinants of desired outcomes. Researchers review literature to discover cause and effect, a research endeavor that is critical to the process of identifying best practices. Activity is built upon explanations. Consequently, programs are the outworking of those explanations or theories. Given theoretical connections, variables that may be manipulated become the point of focus for program development. The key elements to be examined include the diversity of objectives; the relation between functional design and stated objectives; and, the diversity of subpart functions performed by the entire organizational network.

Because the statement of goals and objectives is theory based, it is imperative that one specify in measurable terms what the goal is. Then, one must review the literature and other information to determine what contributes and what prohibits the presence of the desired goal.

Figure 2.1 – Problem Response Formulation

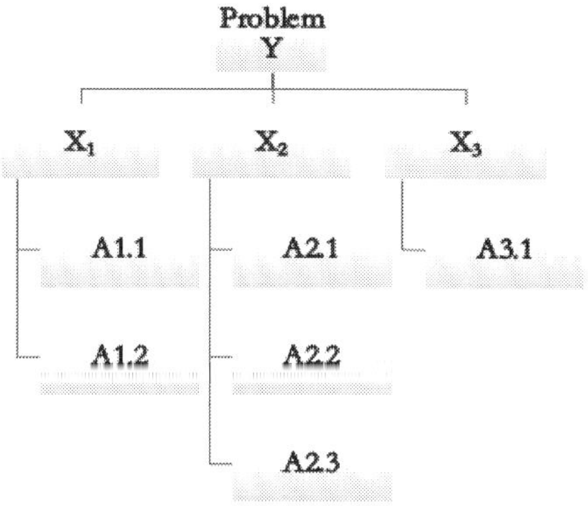

Problem
Y

X_1 X_2 X_3

A1.1 A2.1 A3.1

A1.2 A2.2

A2.3

$A_1 + \ldots + A_N$ = Treatment (T) referred to as X_T for intervention

Once you have completed your inventory of organizations (Chapter 1 exercise), the next step is to identify at least one crucial sector of the community, that which provides the greatest amount of leverage in relation to quality of life. This may be done as a consequence of conducting a SWOT analysis. With an understanding of the Strengths/Weaknesses/Opportunities/Threats confronting the jurisdiction, you may:

Step 1--Gain access to the information required to enhance economic development activity;

Step 2--Conduct a Systematic Literature Review to glean an account of the state of knowledge on the leverage area. The idea is to present what is known about that topic and in doing identify where gaps in knowledge exist that may have implications for jurisdiction. Obviously, that leverage point as a research topic must be stated with precision, narrowly so that you make an exhaustive review of options. Narrow statement does not mean shallow. Your search must be pursued with strategic intent, approached in an effort to find out elements that prove critical, the knowledge of which can make a significant difference in the quality of life in the community. There are at least three commonly encountered yet distinct approaches (and even more if you care to look for them) - approaches that one may take to systematically review the literature on areas challenging the community with the goal of ultimately bringing to bear informed recommendations for improvement. You may approach your leverage topic:

(1) *Chronologically*---That is, from the perspective of the historical progression of understanding of your topic over time; or,

(2) *Assembly of Emerging Information*---That is, identify an aspect of your topic that is relatively new and then finding out what authors are currently saying about this new attribute (innovation/prototype/pilot). With this approach, I suggest that you organize your thinking around answering the question, "What Works?" or, finally,

(3) *Interdisciplinary Pursuit*—This is where you identify how the pressing issue confronting the jurisdiction in its generic form is handled by the various disciplines, examining transferable functional components and strategies, citing what authors from each discipline suggest are the key aspects that may be applied in present circumstances.

Questions for assessing what works should guide your review of the literature. Aspects include:

-- Determining the likelihood of occurrence, the probability of Success/Failure

-- Determining standards and best approaches to quality control (often in the realm of parametric procedures)

-- Drawing well-reasoned conclusions from limited information, through the use of Sampling/Bayesian procedures and modifying predictions based upon observations

-- Exploring scenarios based upon uncertainty through the use of risk perception and decision-making methods

-- Exploring scenarios based upon past performance by monitoring Frequency of occurrence of specified outcomes and documenting event histories

-- Examining differences in expected and observed quite possibly through the use of nonparametric procedures

-- Examining definition of terms, terms defined by whom, with what assumptions attached, and in what context

-- Identifying the administrative perspective via the collection of Public Administrator Generated Information often associated with planning

-- Identifying trends [*Generalized Least Square/Regression Modeling*]

-- Comparing two or more groups [*Parametric and Non-Parametric Procedures*]

-- Determining how configurative cases relate to each other [*Network Analysis*][12]

-- Determining under what conditions, if any there are significant differences between systemic cases[13]

-- Determining the potential consequences for cases if certain actions are taken [*Systematic Literature Review*]

-- Determining the likely consequences for cases if specific variables are modified [*Simulations*]

Given the presence of a theoretical relation between programmatic strategy and outcome, the evaluation criteria for acceptable programmatic performance may be established. This measure is contingent upon appropriate implementation of the programmatic design. The criteria can establish expected outcome parameters providing quality control measures for formative and summative or "impact" evaluation.

The issue of expected versus actual result becomes more sophisticated with the use of counterfactuals that serve as a baseline comparison of activity effect so that the difference in outcome attributable to intervention can be determined. Those who are familiar with the work of Mohr (1995) are aware of the evaluative logic behind the use of the multichannel approach to evaluation. [14] This approach consists of handling of all aspects of

---

[12] For a thorough presentation of social network analysis, see Stanley Wasserman and Joseph Galaskiewicz .(eds.) 1994. *Advances in Social Network Analysis*. Thousand Oaks: Sage Publications. As an introduction see: David Knoke and James H. Kuklinski. *Network Analysis*. Newbury Park, Calif. [u.a.]: Sage Publ, 2002.

[13]See Adam Przeworski and Henry Teune. *The Logic of Comparative Social Inquiry*. New York: Wiley-Interscience, 1970.

[14] Mohr, Lawrence B. *Impact Analysis for Program Evaluation*. Thousand Oaks, Calif: Sage Publications, 1995.

a problem, either as reflected in the mission statement of an agency, or in a publicly mandated document requiring functional coordination, or as a cluster of agencies specified, all answering to one body or coordinated collection of entities and having centralized administration. The multi-channel approach is in accordance with this operational definition and requires the review of structure that implementation takes, the result of either the specificity or the implementation of policy.

Given the nature of the configurative structure, what must be monitored is: rates of dissolution of network subparts/functions; concentration of service type; the number of network subpart functions and the resulting impact.

Of course, the dominant question that emerges from the variables and subjective analysis offered here would be, —What constitutes progress in the midst of disaster response and its aftermath activities? Perceptions of amelioration will need to avoid the pitfalls posed by individual difference often associated with piecemeal and fragmented strategies. More importantly, policy makers and analysts will have to meet the challenge of relational commonality and comprehensiveness in prescribing implementation preventive strategies. This will require changed analogy from humanistic to that of mechanistic, with a focus on function in many cases. But a more fundamental change would be to exercise wisdom concerning the human condition as means of isolating true causal relations. Undetected, such may work havoc in the midst of societal calamity.

Collaborative Stewardship

The accountability orientation entails the itemization of objectives of operation at all levels of program execution. It requires the determination of prerequisites for optimal operation and the development and subsequent measure of absolute standards of efficiency and effectiveness. The accountability measured is that of decision-makers and designees at various operational levels of the organization. The product of this activity would be the structural and functional characteristics of the operation under review; factors determining the direction in which the entity is evolving; and the degree to which the operative collaborating entity has been able to reach implied and specifically mandated goals/objectives as well as those set operationally by the decision-maker. The evaluation process follows the above from a discrepancy orientation – that is, to what degree does the actual deviate from plan in relation to:

· Designed organization versus actual operation;

· Expected versus observed performance; and,

· Planned versus observed linkages between functional entities required to achieve of specified goals

To measure discrepancy, the issue of accountability is present in the

· Itemization of objectives at all operational levels;

· Determination of the prerequisites of the operation; and,

· Development of absolute standards of efficiency and effectiveness

· Extent that the operation is multi-channeled for change.

In the case where many activities or operations are underway to achieve aspects of the same goal, it is necessary to determine the comprehensive nature of the initiative. These measures involve determining: 1) to what degree the initiative is shaped by pre-existing structure/function characteristics; 2) to what degree is consolidation, dissolution, longevity/latitude, and point of initiation having an impact on the effectiveness of the implementation structure; and, if comprehensiveness is the result; 3) to what degree did decisive planning strategy or series of documentable factors render the current outcome levels.

Table 2.1A Multi-Channel Operations: Collaborative Implementation Variables[15]

L	=	Longevity of Operations
Pc	=	Program Components
Ff	=	Functions-Frequency
Fd	=	Functional Diversity
Cu	=	Consolidated Units (Number)
Cud	=	Consolidated Units (Diversity)
P/dr	=	Plan/Development Ratio
P/dr/ps	=	Plan/Development Ratio to Political Solvency
P	=	Point of Consolidation
Cw	=	Crosswalk Measure of Validity: Implementation/Mission
I	=	Intermittency Rate

Measuring configurative impact of individual and collective intervention initiatives, the consequences of configurative change, the critical areas of coverage, the degree of coverage compared to scope of problem, points of leverage examined while incorporating the use of social network applications to formative and summative evaluation; and, the use

[15] See Olivia Hidalgo-Hardeman. 1993. "Evaluating Social Service Delivery Configurations. "*Evaluation Review*. 17, no. 6: 603-20.

nonparametric procedures in the measurement of configurative impact requires connecting the dots between perceived adversity and the respective cause. Then, with explanation for the existence of malady, the most appropriate response should be derived for eliminating the problem (or *at a minimum, the containment of the problem and/or its rate of increased severity.*) With that information, analytical methods may be used to determine the necessary configuration of response, the required rate of consolidated cooperation; the required rate of multi-level/interagency collaborative activity that should be pursued; and, the nature of regional cooperation should it be determined that the nature of the problem such a scope of collaborative intervention. Care should be given to monitor community support for initiatives including the rate of change in the rate of change in perceptions among vulnerable populations.

Table 2.1B Multi-Channel Operations: Collaborative Implementation Variables & Political Solvency Variables

Lc	=	Leadership Change
Ig	=	Income Gap
S	=	Rate of Subsistence
Dg	=	Disruptive Element Intensity
Sc	=	Spatial Character
C/P	=	Concentration/Propensity for Disruptive Element
SD	=	Service Disruption---Infrastructure
AM	=	Adaptive Mechanism (Type)
IA	=	Institutional Adaptation Rate
TA	=	Threshold of Acceptability
CC	=	Culture Change
DS	=	Demographic Shift
PP	=	Political Polarization
ID	=	Institutional Dimensions
EE	=	Exodus Effect
Pov	=	Proportion of Population Impoverished
Pov1	=	Severity of Poverty
Pov2	=	Geographic Concentration
Pov3	=	Intermittency Rate
Pov4	=	In-Migration Rate
Pov5	=	Poverty Births
SDI	=	Societal Disengagement
BC	=	Behavioral Character
HV	=	Health Vulnerability
SV	=	Social Vulnerability---Crime, etc.
CD	=	Chemical Dependency Rate

In preparation for the possibility of natural or man-made disaster, collaborating stewards should monitor the configuration's intervention capacity given a full array of scenarios. Thought should be given to cultivating a regional and even global configurative partnerships prepared to respond to specific types of maladies for which the individual jurisdiction may be ill-equipped to address. This assessment well in advance of any cataclysmic event may prove valuable to the aftermath during the quest for normalcy.

Table 2. 1.C Inventory of Organizations

Panoramic View Questions to Consider

Q1	What organizations make up the current configuration of services/activities conducted in the community?
Q2	What functions are performed by the network of organizations present in your area?
Q3	What are the consequences that result from the current configuration of services?
Q4	Are there any known adverse consequences that exist as a byproduct of the current configuration of services/organizational arrangements?
Q5	*If yes to Q4*, what impact do those adverse consequences have on the community?
Q6	Are those negative traits concentrated or otherwise most prominent in select/problematic/or otherwise critical locations within the jurisdiction?
Q7	What consequences might occur if changes were made in the nature of organizational coverage for those locations?
Q8	How much does the current configuration cost?
Q9	What is the cost-benefit ratio of the configuration?
Q10	Does the configuration selective diminish benefits that would otherwise be gleaned?
Q11	What is the impact of the topology or sequence of services rendered across the jurisdiction?
Q12	What would the optimal configuration of organizations look like for the promotion of life in the community?

Typically, the analytical methods associated with public policy include not only statistics but modeling strategies. The topics are as follows:

Defining problem situation
Identifying objectives
Identifying constraints
Defining preferences
Identifying options
Measuring growth
Systems analysis
Forecasting and simulation
Population projection
Discounting
Annualizing
Cost-Benefit analysis
Cost-effectiveness analysis
Linear programming
Decision analysis
Computer simulation
Waiting Line Models
Markov processes
Sensitivity analysis
Scenario analysis
Subjective probability assessment

The above methods plus statistical techniques will be useful for assessing options for a myriad of issues that confront our nation.

Table 2.2 Matrix of Evaluation Design and Statistical Methodology

Evaluative Research Strategies	*General Description*	*Evaluative Question Designed to Answer*	*Statistical Methodology/Strategy*
Needs Assessment	Interviews/Questionnaire	What needs to be done? What problems exist?	Decision Analysis/ Subjective Probability
Implementation Analysis	Formative Evaluation	Is the program(s) executed according to design?	Measure the extent to which implementation was carried out
Program Monitoring Techniques	Quality Control Techniques Discrepancy/Managerial Audit	How well are the program components operating? (Product) Are there management activities that adversely affect the [illegible] program? (Process)?	Effect measurement Process assessment and treatment assessment (matching activity to desired effect)
Randomized Experiments	Complete Randomization Single Grouping/Randomized Block Design Double Grouping/Latin Squares Design Cross-over Designs Random-Comparison Group Design	Can a desired outcome be attributed to the presence of a specified intervention? (Treatment allotted on the basis of change.)	ANOVA/ANCOVA/Regression

Table 2.2 Matrix of Evaluation Design and Statistical Methodology ***Cont.***[16]

Regression Discontinuity	Assignment rule is known; randomization is not applied. Groups are not equivalent and hence require adjustment for comparison.	How much benefit is actually gleaned from exposure to the program by a limited number of pool qualified for participation. (Benefit: avoids perception of favoritism.)	Regression (Score above or equal to specified value. This value will be based on a pretreatment measure that divides groups. Those that have a value below the cut-point will not.)
Randomized Comparative Change	Pre-Posttest Design and Untreated Control Group	Given a point of comparison with similar cases, how much changed status may be attributed to intervention?	Regression
Nonequivalent Control Group Design	Trend Analysis	Is there a significant difference between pre and posttest?	Regression Adjustment Change Score Analysis
Interrupted Time Series Design	Trend Analysis	How much change in trend status of a phenomenon may be attributed to the intervention?	Regression or ARIMA (Auto Regressive, Integrated Moving Average)
Post-Only Correlational Design	Selection Decentralized	What is the relationship between the degree of exposure to a treatment and the value of the desired outcome?	Correlation and Regression
Benefit-Cost Analysis	Price willing to pay is used as a measure of the relative value of activities	Is the amount of benefit derived worth the cost of intervention when compared to other possible alternatives?	Extrapolation and imputing value of payment to the utility.
Multi-Attribute Evaluation	Decision research tool for determining what actions should take place as a result of the evaluation.	How do stakeholders perceive the performance of the intervention?	Decision Analysis
Sub-objective Design	Scriven's Modus Operandi (MO) Method	What is the nature of the relation between intervention, sub-objectives, and the outcome?	Recursive structural equation "presumptive reasoning."

Evaluative Issues Associated with Collaboration

The Evaluation Equation will consist of the following structure:

The X variables are representative of the outcome line sub objective and task activities. Paradigm attributes for collaborative initiatives across jurisdictions would entail the following.

Theory-based by Sector and Collective Problem

Each element in the equation will be present on the basis of what is known about the

[16] Based upon Lawrence B. Mohr. *Impact Analysis for Program Evaluation*. Thousand Oaks, Calif: Sage Publications, 1995.

causal relation between the presence of Y (where Y is outcome, either desired or that which is problematic) and a variety of X's (where X represents either that which explains the presence of Y or otherwise an essential component for desired outcome, Y).[17]

Ex. 1.2 Accommodates planning via simulation Markov processes may be used to determine the direction in the configuration of collaborative activity is moving

Ex. 1.3 Anticipates change in conditions using graphical models for multivariate statistics, one may map the consequences of change given the dynamic characteristics of the X variables.

Ex. 1.4 Facilitates projection of impact if any subpart is manipulated. Collective analysis of the X variables, when incorporated into a forecasting model, may be simulated. Structural equation models involve more than one dependent variable; involve more than one equation; and, involve some dependencies among the variables.

S and Y are dependent variables;

But, S serves also as an independent variable.

The model is recursive when dependent variables are not mutually dependent and not spuriously related by some omitted cause.[18] Variables are measured in chronological sequence.

---

[17] An example of X representing essential components can be seen in Decisions and Designs Inc. McLean VA, Fischhoff, Baruch; Slovic, Paul; and Lichtenstein, Sarah. *Fault Trees: Sensitivity of Estimated Failure Probabilities to Problem Representation*\. 1977.
<http://oai.dtic.mil/oai/oai?&verb=getRecord&metadataPrefix=html&identifier=ADA057163>.

[18] *Op. Cit*, Mohr, p. 187.

S may affect Y, but Y is not affecting S. There is not a feedback loop.

Sub-Objective Methods

By decomposing into two or more chained causal links, we are looking for:

----Magnitude of relationship;

----Causal proximity

----- So, Sub-objectives(S):

- May be additive within the equation and not dependent on one another;
- May be interactive and therefore multiplicative within the equation for Y and not dependent on each other; and,
- May be chained, that is, dependent on one another so that each appears as a sub-objective in the equation of the one that follows.

Validation Log

If we know S Yields Y, then we need only implement some T(Treatment) that affects S to have the desired outcome.

Note: If magnitude is appreciable, the treatment is operating through another channel in addition to the measured S.

Link: S is designed to address proposed cause of Y. The S may be partially spurious when it is not a part of the treatment in a quasi-experimental sense.

- S scores are not necessarily centralized. Spurious factors may also influence y. Therefore, they may be partially or even completely spurious.

- S may be the true cause of Y.

The link is quasi-experimental to the extent T may cause S. It is important to examine the magnitude or strength of the relation.

Causal proximity is used as another basis of confirming that there is no intervention between J and k.

Example: Enforcement of seat belt use seen in relation to accident fatality as a preventive action.

For relation with sub-objectives to determine link, use statistical significance in measuring magnitude.

Interpretation:

If either bT^1 or bS is unimpressive then either, the treatment operated through another path undefined via sub-objectives or, history or selection effects rendered the results of observed relation.

Analysts must measure and include in the system of equations all of the important channels through which T affects Y.

Where no other channels exist:

$bT = 0$; Summative correlation coefficient

$rTY = (r/TS)\ (r/SY)$

which may have implications for component links. Size of relation is the focus for link between T and S. Examples where the link between T and S maybe established would include monitoring of improved quality of life may have *as determining factors:*

-- Level of citizen influence on decision making in the jurisdiction;

-- Organizational proximity to leverage issue area

-- Direct and indirect implications of individual and organizational programmatic activity in the jurisdiction/community.

Where there is an apparent absence of good governance in the jurisdiction, collaborative stewards should:

--Monitored indicators

--Monitor threats to the resiliency against physical threats on the population with regard to governability and degree of capacity maintained, monitor the status of the presence of governance as opposed to lawlessness.

Goal coordination requires both development and implementation which will include identifying the number of critical points of intervention along with frequency and type of purposeful interaction in the carrying out of needed functions.

Chapter 2 – A Closing Note

The critical point to remember is this: Accurate, truthful (meaning, not partially true) description and explanation for current conditions is essential as such should drive action. Let's move forward to Exercise 2 in the identification of functions formed between organizations.

EXERCISE 2 – FUNCTIONS PERFORMED BETWEEN ORGANIZATIONS

Here are the steps:

2.1. Prepare to conduct a SWOT Analysis by first understanding Social Network Analysis [SNA] which allows you to see organizational stakeholders as having position and interaction within a configuration of organizational interests, each of which has implications for your jurisdiction/community.

2.2 Select a problem identified during the SWOT analysis, a weakness or threat for which a sector dominates in terms of responsibility.

2.3 Map the configuration of exchange associated with that sector using Social Network

Analysis (SNA) to organizational configuration.

2.4 Identify the relationship type of each entity within the sector network.

2.5 Rank entities on the basis of influence within the sector with regard to other entities with that sector.

2.6 Rank entities on the basis of scope of stewardship responsibility over the community with regard to a very specific problem area.

SUGGESTED READING

SNA Considered

Freeman, Linton C., and Douglas R. White. *Research Methods in Social Network Analysis*. New Brunswick, NJ <etc.>: Transaction Publishers, 1992.
2.2-Sectors

SNA Methodological Limits

Hanneman, Robert A. and Mark Riddle. *Introduction to social network methods.* Riverside, CA: University of California, Riverside.2005. (Published in digital form at http://faculty.ucr.edu/~hanneman/)

SNA - Exchange

Real T., Alejandra and Nicolas D. Hasanagas. 2005. "Complete Network Analysis in Research of Organized Interests and Policy Analysis: Indicators, Methodical Aspects and Challenges." *Connections*, 26(20: 89-106.

Relationship Type and SNA

Cawson, Alan. *Corporatism and Political Theory*. New York: Basil Blackwell Inc. 1986.

Wolfe, Alvin W. 2005."Connecting the Dots without Forgetting the Circles." *Connections*, 26(2): 107-119.

SNA - Influence

Processes in a Longitudinal Study of Friendship Groups and Risk-Taking". *Connections,* 25(2): 59-76.

Collaborative Stewardship

Pituch, K. A., T. A. Whittaker, and W. Chang. 2016. "Multivariate Models for Normal and Binary Responses in Intervention Studies". *American Journal of Evaluation.* 37, no. 2: 270-286.

Stewardship Responsibility

O'Toole, L. J.1997. "The Implications of Democracy in a Networked Bureaucratic World." *Journal of Public Administration Research and Theory,* 7(3), 443-459.

O'Toole, Laurence J. 2004. "The Theory-Practice Issue in Policy Implementation Research". *Public Administration.* 82, no. 2: 309-329.

3

CONTEXTUAL FACTORS YIELDING RESPONSE VERSUS INDIFFERENCE

"Whoever stops up his ears at the cry of the poor will himself cry, but not be answered.
Proverbs 21:13, *Holy Bible*, CJB

-

Indicators of Success. Thresholds of Acceptability. Evaluability. Vehicles for Improvement. Transparency. Collaborative Effort.

By taking a clinical approach to economic development by first diagnosing the development problems; and, then finding what can be done to minimize the scope and severity of the problem(s) identified, useful information may be prepared as a report suitable for public sector decision makers and other stakeholders.

Our goal is to conduct evidence-based research in order to find out what has been documented as having worked in comparable jurisdictions, locations that once experienced and have now recovered from the problems currently plaguing the jurisdiction under examination. And, if the jurisdiction has no overt economic development or severe quality of life problems, then the goal will be to discover what it would take to make your good location great.

Consider the following steps:

Collaborative Stewardship

1. Identify the key problems/weaknesses and/or underutilized opportunities present in your jurisdiction. A key problem for this exercise would be any challenge that if it were minimized or eliminated fixed would result in other (secondary) issues becoming less problematic.
2. Identify potential problem areas you may have discovered as a consequence of conducting a needs assessment of community based upon available social indicators.[19]
3. Identify trends.
4. Develop an index of vulnerability
5. Establish a vulnerability score for each census tract within the community.
6. Examine population density.
7. Determine scope and severity of problem within the jurisdiction.

Establishing Connections – A Preemptive Move to Restoration in the Event of a Disaster: Proposed Conceptual Framework & Methodology for Collaborative Stewardship

What follows is a description of spillover effects of disasters to which joint response may require. Examine what that dynamic means for resource management in the event of not only a single but also multiple simultaneous calamities.

[19]See U.S. Census information: https://www.census.gov/geo/maps-data/data/tiger-data.html

MILITARY-CIVILIAN AND OTHER LARGE SCALE COLLABORATIVE STEWARDSHIP CONSIDERATIONS

First, organizational self-assessments should be instituted and then be immediately followed by organizational reputational assessments. This information then could be transferred into a layered projection of concentric circles that reflect relative distance from the problematic center rather than simply relative Social Network Analysis (SNA) distances from each other.[20] As a planning device, a scale that reflects thresholds of acceptability performance that pictorially places organizations in mutually agreed upon position to absorb need. Then, the configuration can be monitored on the basis of that united view to determine compliance across network organizations, and functionality of relations between those organizations. Nonparametric indicators unconventionally applied can supplement our understanding of pecking order in response to crisis. What makes this approach unique is that instead of focusing on who communicates or otherwise exchanges with whom in a network, the point of focus becomes what must be prepared for and what configuration of collaborative response given the combination of organizations in existence can maximize the survivability of whole populations while minimizing cost. In that way, SNA then becomes a means for thinking about and then monitoring conformity to planned operations.

Discussion of the points of vulnerability: natural, man-made, and /or civil are now

[20] See Olivia Hidalgo-Hardeman, 1993. "Evaluating Social Service Delivery Configurations," *Evaluation Review: A Journal of Applied Social Research*, Volume 17, Number 6.

under scrutiny. The military/civilian response capabilities review. Eagerly sought is a strategy for integrated effort that relies on the organizational strength within and between nations. There are bumps in the road: political hurdles, prevailing economic realities, and a general lack of zeal for preventive action. From the perspective of natural disaster and recovery, those key areas of import include the general features of disaster response:

I. Risks that Natural Disaster Impose [Covered by Lessons Learned Reports]

II. Risks that Enemy Forces Impose Against:

a. Humanitarian Personnel
b. Community
c. Environment in the form of eco-violence
d. Public Services
e. Civic Operations
f. Law Enforcement

A Brief Example of Equations Associated with Risks that Natural Disaster Impose:

Plenty of information exists on the nature of disasters and relative susceptibility by geographical area. What has been missing is how to incorporate that information into the assessment of collaborative linkage. Given recent studies on vulnerability of at least one Latin American nation, the following equations were developed by Dao and Peduzzi to determine risk. The specific indicators identified and their equations appear below:

According to H. Dao and Pascal Peduzzi of Geneva, the following equations are relevant for the evaluation of human risk and vulnerability to natural disasters.

$$R = H_p \cdot Pop \cdot Vul$$

Where: R = *number of expected human impacts [killed/year]*

H_p = *frequency of a given hazard [event/year]*

Pop = *population living in a given exposed area [population affected/event],*

Vul = *vulnerability depending on socio-economic factors [no units].*

For combined hazard and exposed population, the equation is as follows:

$$R = PhExp \cdot Vul$$

Where,

R = *risk of human losses*

Vul = *population vulnerability*

PhExp = *average number of people exposed to a hazard type by year*

For vulnerability proxy from past events

$$Vul = Risk/PhEXp$$

Where: vulnerability proxy equals the average number of deaths per exposed people

For vulnerability that includes sociopolitical factors:

$$K = C \cdot (PhExp)^a \cdot V_1^{a1}, V_1^{a2}, \ldots, V_1^{an}.$$

Where: K is the number of persons killed by a certain hazard

C is a multiplicative constant

$PhExp^{a}$ *is the physical exposure*

V_1 *are the socio-economic variables*

a_1 *are the exponents of* V_1 *(which can be negative).*[21]

For the calculation of specific natural disaster vulnerability patterns for cyclones, droughts, earthquakes, and floods; variables included in those equations are percentage of urban growth, normalized Gross Domestic Product per capita as purchasing power parity; local density which Dao and Peduzzi define as the population affected divided by the area affected; numbers killed, physical exposure to the natural calamity, transformed value of percentage of arable land, and a transformed value of Human Development Index.

A Small Sample of What Network-Wide Response Equations to Minimize Risks Posed by Enemy Forces: Impact Evaluation Using SNA

Given all that has before, one point remains. The merger of risk information with the network-wide configuration designed to respond to calamity by taking a functional approach to collaborative linkages. A good place to begin is with the flow of funds. Funding source dependency and expenditure/priority are presented as ratios. In no way should inquiry rest only on flow of funds. The exhaustive examination would cover all relevant variables discussed earlier in this article. Then the information should be approached with the following variables in mind:

- Concentration of service type (CST) Military and Civilian
- Number of network subpart functions (NSF) Military and Civilian

---

[21] According to Dao and Peduzzi, Taking the logarithms in the vulnerability equation that incorporates sociopolitical factors the equation would be $\ln(K) = \ln(C) + a\ln(PhExp) + a_1 \ln(V_1) + a_2 \ln(V_2) + \ldots + a_p \ln(V_p)$. *These authors go on to discuss the need for transformation of variables expressed as percentages so that all variables range between minus and plus infinity. See Hy Dao, Pascal Peduzzi, "Global evaluation of human risk and vulnerability to natural hazards," Enviro-info 2004, Sh@ring, Editions du Tricorne, Geneve, ISBN 282930275-3, vol. I, p. 435-446.*

- Number (rate) of additions to subpart functions [ASF] Military and Civilianr
- Number (rate) of subpart consolidations [SC] Military and Civilian
- Point of union of diverse/similar subparts [UDS/USS] Military and Civilian

Equations that might initiate such an examination would include:

$$NWC + ND + V \rightarrow RO$$

Where,

NWC is the network wide configuration of military and civilian actors

Where NWC is based upon

ND is the nature of the disaster

V is the Vulnerability based upon Dao and Peduzzi series of equations

RO represents the immediate disaster response outcomes for monitoring

impact of existing collaborative linkages.

Close vigilance of the above will allow the identification of fractures in collaborative response.

Now, there are quite a few software facilitated measures available to examine the nature of o between actors.[22]

We have good reason to believe that analytical strategies such as that offered by social network analysis coupled with other heuristics may assist us in our

[22] Software for Social Network Analysis by Mark Huisman of Heymans Institute/DPMG, Marijtje A.J. van Duijn ICS/Statistics & Measurement Theory, University of Groningen,3rd October 2003. See http://stat.gamma.rug.nl/snijders/Software%20for%20Social%20Network%20Analysis%20CUP_ch13_Oct2003.pdf for a convenient summary of SNA related software.

understanding of linkages within and between international stakeholders.

The goal is not simply to document what is, but to also prescribe what should be. Attention should be given to the ultimate development of a security compliance system that is not only effective at keeping enemies at bay, but also supports as priority the maintenance of the delicate balance between national sovereignty and international intervention. To develop the compliance system, as indicated by the full variety of elements generic to configurations at large, a number strategic areas of vulnerability will be added to the list. These along with candid assessments of capacity building within and across borders of municipalities, counties, states and regions must be taken into consideration.

In summary, the application of evaluative logic discussed briefly in this book rests on a basic notion which is this. **If frequency of contact should reflect levels of strategic (meaning functional) interdependence, we can compare the patterns of contact within and between organizations to known requisite levels of interdependence predicated upon the position of each organization/entity or subunit within configurative network of exchange.**

Although the goal of evaluation is to determine the extent to which policy outcomes may be attributed to programmatic intervention, one must develop statements that serve to describe a critical test of the credibility of explanation such that at issue is the relation between the program and/or programmatic components and the presence of a measurable outcome. In theory, the programmatic aspects should be seen either as contributing to the presence of a favorable outcome or minimizing the presence of an adverse outcome. The empirical statements may serve as critical tests of the credibility of each argument justifying action. In addition, one should be clear about what one expects to find as a result of examining the outcomes of these tests. These anticipated results are empirical consequences. If the empirical statements prove to be true, then the theory (explanation) for the presence of a specific outcome has credibility. If a series of varied empirical statements that test the theory in question shown to be true, then the theory demonstrates even greater credibility[23]. Alternative explanations require examination.

Chapter3 – A Closing Note

We must pray to rightly assess situations. False conclusions about reality can yield wrong action, inappropriately rationalized. Also, it must be further reinforced in our thinking that organizations exist to serve individuals for they collectively constitute the community. This last point is not an inconsequential. To the degree that the term "community" is seen as absolving entities from the role of stewards operating in the best interest of each individual, action plans will ineffective at securing community well-being. Indeed, such absolution may become the breeding ground for increased disparity, inequity, and overall vulnerability to adverse conditions.

EXERCISE 3 - MAPPING CURRENT CONFIGURATION

Create a display of the Social Network Analysis (SNA) generated configuration. Depict the relationship between entities with regard to shared:

3.1 Information Exchange

---

[23] See: Arthur L Stinchcombe. *Constructing Social Theories*. Chicago: University of Chicago Press. 1987.

Collaborative Stewardship

3.2 Shared Clientele and Sequentially Exchanged Clientele

3.3 Shared Funding Source and Funding Source Dependency

3.4 Reputational Hub

SUGGESTED READING

SNA Methods & Applications

Burt, Ronald S., and Michael J. Minor. *Applied Network Analysis: A Methodological Introduction.* Beverly Hills: Sage Publications, 1983.

Honeycutt, Todd C., and Debra A. Strong. 2012. "Using Social Network Analysis to Predict Early Collaboration Within Health Advocacy Coalitions". *American Journal of Evaluation.* 33, no. 2: 221-239.

Carley, Kathleen M. et. al. 2002. "Destabilizing Networks." *Connections* 24(3): 79-92.

Castells, Manuel. *The Rise of the Network Society.* Malden: Blackwell Publishers. 2000. Marsden P.V., and Campbell K.E. 2012. "Reflections on Conceptualizing and Measuring Tie Strength". *Social Forces.* 91, no. 1: 17-23.

Honeycutt, Todd C., and Debra A. Strong. 2012. "Using Social Network Analysis to Predict Early Collaboration Within Health Advocacy Coalitions". *American Journal of Evaluation.* 33, no. 2: 221-239.

Marsden P.V., and Campbell K.E. 2012. "Reflections on Conceptualizing and Measuring Tie Strength". *Social Forces.* 91, no. 1: 17-23.

Wasserman, Stanley and Joseph Galaskiewicz .(eds.) 1994. *Advances in Social Network Analysis.* Thousand Oaks: Sage Publications.

Funnell, S. C. *2000. "Developing and Using a Program Theory Matrix for Program Evaluation and Performance Monitoring". NEW DIRECTIONS FOR EVALUATION. no. 87: 91-102.*

4

COMMON OPERATING PICTURE SPECIFYING WHO DOES WHAT, HOW, WHEN AND WHY

"The Word of the Lord came to me saying, 'What do you see, Jeremiah?' And, I said 'I see a rod of an almond tree.' Then the LORD said to me, 'You have seen well, for I am watching over my word to perform it." ---Jeremiah 1:11, *Holy Bible*, NAS

-

Main Conversation. Systematic Literature Review. Evidence-based Research. Structural Imagery. Outcome Minded. Network Fragmentation. Parameters for Evaluation.

It is important to understand the events that shaped the current configuration of stakeholders in the community. Events tend to shape conversation.

1. *Major Events* – A timeline with a very brief description of the event and its significance for the current state of affairs in the area.
2. *Major Actors* -- A list of key figures for the geographical area and a brief description of their role, policy position, affiliations, and general significance to current area conditions.
3. *Major Issues* – A prioritized list of the significant controversies confronting the area.
4. *Turning Points* – Itemized list of strategic turning points, or points of decision that led to current conditions in the jurisdiction/community.
5. *Lessons Learned* – Identify lessons learned from strategic intervention into this problem region.
6. *Implications for Security* – List what the area situation means for law enforcement and

general security for the jurisdiction/community.

7. *Parameters of Organizational Response* – List the constraints associated collaborative options for the area.

8. *Projected Future* – Given past trends, what do experts suggest the trajectory of future events to be in the region?

9. *Ways Monitored* – How do members of the Intelligence Community currently monitor key indicators in the area?

10. *How to Measure Overall Impact* – What approach is currently being used to measure impact of intervention efforts?

Interviews may be conducted to uncover the answer to the above questions along with other pertinent information. See Exhibit A at the end of this chapter.

Then, given the factors that tend to drive past and present conversation that suggest the causes for the current status of the jurisdiction, the next element of information for maximizing effectiveness in the exercise of collaborative stewardship is to examine best practices in addressing the issues, identification of successful strategies that have worked in locations that confront comparable dynamics. The precursor to this exploration would be the development of a systematic literature review.

Stages Required for Conducting a Systematic Literature Review

Stage 1: Specify Problem

1. Specify the problem in the form of a researchable question. *Note:* The research question must be narrow enough to effectively conduct an exhaustive search of all pertinent aspects of the issue.

2. Your topic of focus should include a statement of both the practical and theoretical significance of your research question.

3. Identify all the pertinent search terms associated with your selected researchable question. Care must be taken to identify what the parameters should be for the investigation of your research question. This decision should reflect a clear understanding of what will be included and excluded from your study.

4. Make sure there is comprehensive balance of views registered in the identification of literature so that works listed are representative of all perspectives. The search for truth requires thorough search without *a priori* bias.

5. Identify the relevant search engines, data bases, and scholarly journal publications to be used in the identification of key voices on the research question.

Stage 2: Literature List

6. Generate your exhaustive list of writings that discuss the pertinent aspects of the research question you have selected.

7. Isolate themes associated with those key terms you used to generate that initial literature list, and do so making special note of thematic contributions made.

8. Make sure that your list of references reflects all of the pertinent works associated with the succinct statement of your research question.

Stage 3: Annotated Bibliography

9. Generate annotations for each of the documents you reviewed to help you answer your research question.

10. Elaborate on points of commonality and difference between the voices on the subject.

11. Identify points of controversy and the implications for arriving at an answer to your research question.

12. Assess the merits of each argument rendered to arrive at points that are indisputable.

Stage 4: Systematic Literature Review Final Report

13. Write a review of the findings generated by your exhaustive review of the literature. This should reflect best practices in solving the problem currently encountered.

14. Then, as a consequence of that exhaustive review of pertinent literature, provide a succinct answer to your research question.

15. Discuss both the practical and the theoretical implications of the answer.

The goal is to develop a common operating picture, that which approximates a snapshot of conditions past and present along with indicators of trajectory will allow collective consideration of the assets and return on investment gleaned from current configuration of response to the challenges confronting the community.

Mapping the configuration for such will enable coordination of capacity building efforts consistent with larger goals of community development

Then, critically analyze community development initiatives and policy proposals, being careful to document prior attempts to resolve adversity.

Chapter4 – A Closing Note

Since it is on the basis of credible explanations offered that must develop our Action plans, deviation from execution of those God-honoring plans is a discrepancy that requires correction. Look for configurative gaps as you complete Exercise 4 in order to determine the level of sufficiency in problem coverage.

EXERCISE 4 – MAPPING PROBLEM COVERAGE

Having completed a SWOT Analysis of the jurisdiction, locate social indicators related to reported weaknesses and threats confronting the jurisdiction.

4.1 Identify trends.

4.2 Develop an index of vulnerability.

4.3 Establish a score for each census tract within the community.

4.4 Examine population density as a principle component of risk assessment.

4.5 Determine scope and severity of problems with the jurisdiction.

SUGGESTED READING

Multi-Attribute Utility Technology/Decision Analysis

Edwards, Ward, and J. Robert Newman. *Multiattribute Evaluation*. Newbury Park, Calif. [u.a.]: Sage, 1993.

Mercado Ramirez, Ernesto. *Tecnicas para la toma de decisiones: la accion mas importante de la activida humana*. Mexico: Limusa, 1991.

Hammond, Kenneth R. and American Association for the Advancement of Science. *Judgment and Decision in Public Policy Formation*. AAAS Selected Symposium 1. Boulder, Colo.: Published by Westview Press for the American Association for the Advancement of Science, 1978.

EXHIBIT A[24]

ADMINISTRATIVE SURVEY OF ORGANIZATIONAL STATUS

DIRECTIONS: This survey instrument should be administered to organizations that have a long history of operation within the jurisdiction/community.

I. Respondent ID

a. Initial Respondent______________________________

b. Position______________________________

c. Organization______________________________

d. Location: ______________________________

e. Phone Numbers: ______________________________

f. Email Address: ______________________________

g. Website: ______________________________

h. Other Contact Persons:

(List names, positions, etc.)

INTERVIEWER NOTES:

II. GOALS/MISSION

[24] Hidalgo-Hardeman, Olivia M. A *Probabilistic Analysis of Social Services Network Failure.* Corpus Christi: Coastal Bend Council of Governments. 1988.

a. When was your organization founded?

b. What is the overall goal of your organization?

c. What is the source of your organization's organizational mandate?

d. How are your services administered?

e. What is your funding source(s)?

f. May we review a breakdown of your expenditures (percent) or have access to a copy of your current operating budget?

Comment:

III. EXTERNAL INFLUENCES, OVERSIGHT, ADVISOR

a. Do you have an advisory board?

   i. Who are the members?

b. How has the organization changed structurally and financially?

   i. What events or milestones represent major changes in the operation and/or demand for your organization?

   ii. How has the clientele being served changed over time?

c. Who are the most significant actors that have influence on the way you provide your services internally and externally?

   i. Do those actors have decision making powers within the organization or do you consider them to be more of a clientele group?

      1. Who has an impact on how your organization runs on a daily basis?

      2. OPTIONAL/ Interviewers Discretion: May we have a copy of job descriptions for those individuals and your procedures manual

IV. SERVICE PROVISION

a. How many persons are being served per week?

b. Are there specific time-periods that stand out as representing changes in eligibility and demand for services? [*Please be specific.*]

c. Do you have what you need to get the job done?

   . *If no, what's needed?*

d. Do you have the resources to meet current demand?

. *If YES, how much increased demand can you effectively handle?*

e. What can go wrong in service delivery?

f. What are the obstacles to service provision?

g. How is outreach conducted?

h. Can you meet current demand?

i. If so, how much increased demand can you effectively handle?

j. What are the obstacles to service expansion?

k. How is outreach conducted?

V. CLIENTELE DATA

a. Do you produce a report of the demographic characteristics of the client institutions served?

b. How often is clientele data updated?

VI. ORGANIZATIONAL INTERACTION

a. With what organizations do you interact? (List here)

i. With what organizations do you interact in the sharing of clientele? (Please list.)

ii. With which organizations do you share information? (Please list.)

iii. With what organizations do you share facilities and/or materials. (Please list.)

VII. PUBLIC POLICY ISSUES CONFRONTING THE JURISDICTION

a. How successful is your organization in achieving its goals?

b. What issues need to be addressed?

c. What questions remain?

d. Do you intend to expand services?

e. What method do you intend to use to deliver services to these additional persons?

f. Do you have concerns about delivering services to certain populations? (Be specific.)

g. Do you already serve any of these populations now? (Discretionary)

h. Are there any organizations or individuals that threaten the success of your organization? If yes, are they linked to Human Trafficking or other transnational crime?

i. Is there any organized crime in the city? (Please be specific.)

j. What impact does law enforcement have on your service operation?

-

PART TWO: *DISCREPANCY*

5

CONFRONTING RESOURCE DISCONTINUITIES

"You shall not have in your bag of differing weights, a heavy and a light. You shall not have in your house differing measures, a large and a small. You shall have a perfect and just weight, a perfect and just measure that your days may be lengthened in the land that the LORD thy God has given you. For all who do such things, all who behave unrighteously, are an abomination to the LORD our God."
---Deuteronomy 25:13-16, *Holy Bible*, NKJV

Network-Wide View. Difference between Organizational Design and Actual Operations. Causal Theory and Collaboration Revisited. Multi-Channel Appropriate Decision-Making.

Is there a significant difference between organizational design and actual operation?

Evaluative questions depend upon metrics that assess summative network-wide transformation impact. With the use of content analysis data both with respect to relationships between stakeholders and with respect to the cognitive maps of individual actors, the practical significance is that the evaluation may identify factors affecting the implementation of programs peculiar to a particular site or timeframe. Additionally, the lineage among factors affecting the implementation strategy and the development of procedures and scales for measuring variations within proposed explanatory variables may receive scrutiny.

Ultimately, the relationship between policy and organization change has two features. The two features of the relationship between organizational and policy change involve the fact that reorganization efforts may prove to be merely cosmetic, not accompanied by changes in the substance of policy. Also, presumed organizational change may involve innovative or terminating elements; and can have "spillover" effects on operations of other organizations.[25] Given the nature the above, it should be understood that there is a need to monitor in concrete terms organizational effort.

Links between Sub-Objectives (*Sn's)* are hypotheses.

Example: Human Trafficking Initiative (Law Enforcement)

Goal: Reduced Transnational Criminal Activity = Y addressed in part by Sub-Objective (S1), increased rate of detection of missing persons.

Counterfactual = Initial measure of slope

Sub-objective Analysis Estimating Equations

$$\textbf{\textit{Eq. 1:}} \quad S_i = a_1 + bT_1 + eS_i$$

This equation shows the T – S link,

where, bT = estimate of the impact of the treatment on the sub-objective.

$$\textbf{\textit{Eq. 2:}} \quad Yi = a + bS\, S_i + bTT_i + eS_i$$

where, bS shows the impact of the sub-objective on the outcome; and, where bT = additional impact of the treatment on the outcome beyond the impact from the sub-objective.[26]

[25] See Hogwood and Peters, 1985

[26] *A Well-Reasoned Response* by Olivia M. McDonald © 2010 – A Limited Access Document.

Methods of sub-objective analysis are based on recursive structural equations.[27]

Structural Equation Models:

- Involve more than one dependent variable;

- Involve more than one equation; and,

- Involve some dependencies among the variables.

- S and Y are dependent variables;

- S is also an independent variable.

By definition, the model is recursive when dependent variables are not mutually dependent and not spuriously related by some omitted cause.

Variables are measured in chronological sequence. S may affect Y, but Y is not affecting S. There is not a feedback loop.

Sub-Objective Methods

T –> S yields Y

With decomposition into two or more chained causal links, we are to look for:

- Magnitude of relationship

[27] Because the analytical approach taken here is one where the focus is on the functions performed in the network, examining the configurative distribution of organizations performing the functions in order to detect deviation from what would be deemed the most appropriate distribution of effort and exchange. Because of the analytical approach outlined in *Collaborative Stewardship*, the methodological challenges are avoided, those which are well explained in the work of Robert A. Hanneman and Mark Riddle. *Introduction to social network methods.*_ Riverside, CA: University of California, Riverside.2005. (Published in digital form at http://faculty.ucr.edu/~hanneman/)

- Causal proximity

Sub-objectives:

- ---May be additive within the equation and not dependent on one another
- ---May be interactive and therefore multiplicative within the equation for and not dependent on each other
- ---May be chained, that is, dependent on one another so that each appears as a sub-objective in the equation of the one that

  Ha the following validation logic applied.

Validation Logic:

Given T → S; and, → S → Y, therefore, T → Y

If we know S determines Y, then we need only implement some T that influences S to have the desired (or more improved) outcome.

Note: *If magnitude is appreciable, the treatment is operating through another channel S_n in addition to the measured S_1.*

S → Y link

-S is designed to address proposed cause of Y. The S may be partially spurious when it is not a part of the treatment in a quasi-experimental sense.

-S scores are not necessarily centralized. Spurious factors may also influence y. Therefore, S→Y may be partially or even completely spurious.

Or, S may be the true cause of Y.

S→Y link is quasi-experimental. Examine the magnitude or strength of the relation. Causal proximity is used as another basis of confirming the status of intervention impact. We return the previous example, *Seat belt use enforcement and the incidence of accident fatality*. For T→Y relation with sub-objectives to determine link, use statistical significance in measuring magnitude. The measures are applied to configuration, either by sector or temporally.

Interpretation:

If either bT^{1} or bS is unimpressive then either,

- ----Treatment operated through another path that is currently undefined via sub-objectives or,
- ----Either history or selection effects rendered the results of observed T → Y relation.

Analysts must include in the system of equations all of the important channels through which T affects Y.

Where no other channels exist:

bT =0; Summative correlation coefficient; and again, rTY = (r/TS) (r/SY) And, again, size of relation is focus for link between T and S.

Of course, the dominant question with regard to amelioration that is facing us in the twenty-first century is, — What constitutes progress? Perceptions of amelioration will need to avoid the pitfalls posed by individual difference, piecemeal and fragmented strategies.

More importantly, policy makers and analysts will have to meet the challenge of relational commonality and comprehensiveness in prescribing policy to ameliorate problems. This will require changed analogy from humanistic to a mechanistic, with focus on function in some cases. But a more fundamental change would be to take a providential on the human condition as means of isolate true cause in the midst societal calamity.

The accountability orientation entails the itemization of objectives of operation at all levels of program execution. It requires the determination of prerequisites for optimal operation and the development and subsequent measure of absolute standards of efficiency and effectiveness. The accountability measured is that of decision-makers and designees at various operational levels of the organization. The product of this activity would be the structural and functional characteristics of the operation under review; factors determining the direction in which the entity is evolving; and the degree to which the operative entity has been able to reach implied and specifically mandated goals/objectives as well as those set operationally by the decision-maker.

The evaluation process follows the above from a discrepancy orientation – that is, to what degree does actual deviate from plan in relation to:

· actual operation;

· observed performance;

·observed linkages between functional entities within and between organizations, thought required to achieve specified goals.

To confront discrepancy, assessment of resources answers the question of whether the building blocks for improvement are available improve conditions.

Given the presence of a theoretical relation between programmatic strategy and outcome, the evaluation criteria for acceptable programmatic performance may be established such that, priority may be assigned to the problem area; and, actors (stakeholders/nations/regions) in essence, all groups associated with the problem and its resolution may be identified.

Chapter5 – A Closing Note

Since it is on the basis of explanations offered that have demonstrated credibility that Action plans should be devised, deviation from execution of those God-honoring plans is a discrepancy that requires correction. Use of analytical tools can drive appropriate consideration of causes of conditions. And, it is on the basis of explanations offered that have demonstrated credibility that Action plans should be devised. Proceed to Exercise 5 - in order to determine the ideal configuration required to address the scope and severity of problems within the jurisdiction[28]

EXERCISE 5 - CONFIGURATIVE RESPONSE PLANNING

5.1 Identify functions most appropriate to serve the community

5.2 Identify percentage of effort required for each census tract given the social indicators

5.3 Identify the scope and sequence of services needed

5.4 Identify the most appropriate resource distribution and by whom

[28] "Ideal" does not automatically assume public sector intervention as required as other approaches may prove more effective.

SUGGESTED READING

Evidence-Based Research
Mental Health Application

Aarons, Gregory A., Michael Hurlburt, and Sarah McCue Horwitz. 2011. "Advancing a Conceptual Model of Evidence-Based Practice Implementation in Public Service Sectors". *Administration and Policy in Mental Health and Mental Health Services Research.* 38, no. 1: 4-23

6

CONFRONTING CAPABILITY DISPARITIES

"*TEKEL.* You have been weighed in the balance and found wanting." ---Daniel 5:27, *Holy Bible*, NIV

-

Strategic analysis. Improvement Requisites. Establishing Definitions of Progress. Measuring Progress. Serving Multiple Entities.

To measure discrepancy, the issue of accountability is ever present in the itemization of objectives at all operational levels the determination of the prerequisites of the operation; and, the development and measure of absolute standards of efficiency and effectiveness.

Once an initiative has been executed, it is necessary to monitor the extent to which operations are performing optimally. To facilitate monitoring, the components that were designed as responses to the problem, should have sub-objectives specified, with each sub-objective linked with indicators of success at the operational level. Standards must be determined based upon the theoretical link between sub-objectives and tasks performed such that exceeding or falling below a certain level will have adverse consequences for the success of the component operations and hence jeopardize the success of the program as a whole. To the extent that the operation is multi-channeled for change, a case where many activities or operations are underway to achieve aspects of the same goal, it is necessary to determine the comprehensive nature of the initiative. This involves determining if the initiative is · shaped by organizational configuration structure/function characteristics; to what degree is consolidation, dissolution, longevity/latitude, and point of initiation having an impact on the effectiveness of the implementation structure; and to determine if comprehensiveness is the result of decisive planning or a series of identifiable factors the absence of which renders the current level of problem.

As mentioned in *Chapter 1*, and then explored using the typical research plan ingredients (Yin, 2003) are now combined. See the following checklist:

□ Identification of principle actors and administrative responsibility

□ Design of organization versus actual operation

□ Determination of the objectives of each operation and the extent of overlap

□ Expected versus observed performance

□ Determination of the degree to which legislative or executive mandate is either stifled or facilitated by the current administrative arrangement

□ Planned versus observed linkages between functional entities within and between organizations required to work collaboratively in the achievement of specified goals

□ Comparison across time changes in the major program requirements along with the itemization of objectives at all operational levels

□ Comparison across time changes in program administrative outputs and the determination of the prerequisites of the operation

□ Comparison across time changes in targeting requirements

the development and measure of absolute standards of efficiency and effectiveness.

To the extent that the operation is multi-channeled for change, a case where many activities or operations are underway to achieve aspects of the same goal, it is necessary to determine the comprehensive nature of the initiative. This involves determining if the initiative is shaped by pre-existing structure/function: to what degree is consolidation, dissolution, longevity/latitude, and point of initiation having an impact on the effectiveness of the implementation structure; and to what degree of comprehensiveness of response/intervention is the result of decisive planning or a series of identifiable factors the absence of which renders the current level of problem.

The practical significance of this approach is that the evaluation may identify factors affecting the implementation of programs peculiar to a particular site or timeframe; linkage among factors affecting the implementation strategy; and development of procedures and scales for measuring variations within proposed explanatory variables. It is especially interesting that these linear policy changes appear to be relatively infrequent, whereas linear changes in organization in the United States appear to be common. This reflects two features of the relationship between organizational and policy change: (1) many reorganizations are cosmetic in the sense that they are not accompanied by changes in the substance of policy, which is maintained in more or less the previous form; (2) although organizational change may involve a simple replacement, accompanying policy changes may be more complex.

Returning to Evaluability, Methodological Processes, and Utilization:

In the discussion of explanation, decision research, judgmental aspects, the detriment x causes y consequence, therefore $X_1, X_2, \ldots, X_n$ should be manipulated to address problem outcome Y. To facilitate our review of this thinking, I offer a model of analysis of public policy decision-making, and the way these decisions have been made a a fundamental level. In addition, a time line is given from beginning of the public policy process with accompanying methodological approaches called as such so that the commonality of response to problem and potential error may be identified. The bottom line of good governance is the protection of inalienable *(meaning, God-given)* rights: life, liberty, and the pursuit of happiness. The reason for government is to put into place mechanisms to secure those rights.[29]

Measuring success involves more than the quality of service delivered, it also requires measuring the extent to which the initiative that is implemented addresses the demand. It is possible to be 100% successful with a program or initiative for which only 20% of the need addressed. Such limited coverage should be detected for a truthful depiction of conditions.

The task is to conduct action research:
Discovering…

a. Criteria by which success may be determined

b. Degree to which success has been attained

[29] *Op. Cit., Well-Reasoned Response*

c. Pockets of failure

d. "Lessons Learned"

Required is an inventory of functions to be performed within the organizational configuration of the community, given the collaborative assessment of need, status, and assessed priorities. The goal is to devise God-honoring economic development capacity building functions collectively.

Chapter 6 – A Closing Note

Faulty explanation hinders progress. Further, to the degree to that correct explanation fails to be linked to action, discrepancy will undermine effort in the community. And, finally, failure to understand and then apply God's word will erode quality of life. For example, failure to recognize that God's word says that it is more blessed to give than to receive opens the door to actions that can be ill-fated. Failure resides in not recognizing the corollary to that statement which is that the inability to contribute is a curse. If that biblical principle were rightly understood, charitable organizations and their collaborators would rethink the end goal of assistance.

EXERCISE 6 – ESTABLISHING THRESHOLDS OF ACCEPTABILITY

6.1 Identify the patterns of need in sequence that characterizes the most vulnerable areas in the community. Be cognizant of Leviticus 26, God's indicators.

6.2 Discover best practices associated with addressing the patterns previously identified.

6.3 Identify the rate of progress normally associated in addressing such patterns, contexts in which progress has been made.

6.4 Establish the criteria for judging rate of progress given the scope and severity of problems in the community.

SUGGESTED READING

Pattern of Need Sequence

Dao, Hy and Pascal Peduzzi. 2004. "Global Evaluation of Human Risk and Vulnerability to Natural Hazards." Enviro-info, Sh@ring, Editions du Tricorne, Geneva, Vol. 1:435-446.

Evidence-based Research on Response to Sequence

Aarons, Gregory A., Michael Hurlburt, and Sarah McCue Horwitz. 2011. "Advancing a Conceptual Model of Evidence-Based Practice Implementation in Public Service Sectors". *Administration and Policy in Mental Health and Mental Health Services Research.* 38, no. 1: 4-23.

Palisano RJ. 2006. "A Collaborative Model of Service Delivery for Children with Movement Disorders: a Framework for Evidence-Based Decision Making". *Physical Therapy.* 86, no. 9: 1295-305.

Outcomes

Earl, Sarah, F. Carden, Michael Quinn Patton, and Terry Smutylo. *Outcome Mapping Building Learning and Reflection into Development Programs.* Ottawa: International Development Research Centre, 2001. <http://www.deslibris.ca/ID/405863>.

Status

McDonald, Olivia M. *Acknowledging God in the Decisions of State: A Treatise on Biblically-Informed Statesmanship.* 2nd Ed. Suffolk, VA: Grace House Publishing, 2015. See God's Indicators on pages 49-50.

PART THREE: *CHANGE*

7

ADDRESSING VULNERABILITIES

"Brothers and Sisters, we urge you to warn those who are lazy. Encourage those who are timid. Take tender care of those who are weak. Be patient with everyone. Make sure no one pays back evil for evil, but always try to do good for each other and for everyone else."
1Thessalonians 5:15-16, *Holy Bible*, LT

-

From Problem Formulation to the Evaluative Action.
Assessment of Operative Theory.
Creating a Common Operating Picture.
Identifying Missing Pieces.

What is required for improvement of quality of life in the community?

To help answer that question, a number of sub-questions should be addressed:

- What has been proposed?
- Is there evidence that what has been proposed will work? And, at what cost?
- What is the required configuration?
- Does that configurative network of organizations currently exist within the community?
- If not, are there obstacles to securing a configurative arrangement that would prove more effective at addressing the needs of the community?
- How should we proceed?
- How should actions be monitored?
- What will constitute the measure of impact?

Collaborative Stewardship

S.W.O.T.--*Strengths, Weaknesses, Opportunities, and Threats*- Analysis conducted on the jurisdiction may render any of (and not be limited to) the following challenges:

Increased Crime/Violence/Gangs

Loss of Industry

High Unemployment

Stagnant Wage Rates

Extreme Poverty

Demographic Shift to Low Income Earners

Large Uneducated/Unskilled Workforce

Sub-Par Educational Opportunities

Absence of Higher Education

Out Migration of College Grads

Aging Population

Large Transient Population

Competing Communities

Inordinate Number of Absentee Landlords

Community/Neighborhood Cleavages

Political Roadblocks/No Strategic Vision/Over Promising Politicians

Heavy Tax Burden

Aging and/or Dilapidated Structure

Location Not Conducive to Commerce

Delayed Disaster Preparedness

Natural Disaster

Man-made Disaster

Environmental Related Issues/EPA/Documented Pollution

Physical Proximity to Nuclear Power Plant(s)

Exposure to Extreme Voltage

Presence of Infectious Disease

Image/Reputation Problems

Poor Public Transportation

Traffic Issues

Lack of Capital Investments

Challenging Highway Logistics/Access

High Rate of Foreclosures

Disproportionate Dependence on Government Programs

Infrastructure Problems

Challenges Associated with Large Military Presence/Shut Down

Out Commuting

Jurisdiction Debt/Bankruptcy

Crippling Tax Structure

Troubling History of Jurisdiction

Public Complacency

Jurisdiction "Not Child- Friendly"

Increased Prevalence of Drugged Sub-Populations

Public Nuisance Locations

By conducting a SWOT Analysis, you are to identify the unique traits of your jurisdiction. *Be specific.* This means that you will have to identify prior attempts to solve the problem(s) and assess the outcomes of those prior attempts so that you will not "reinvent the wheel." Know exactly what went wrong with prior attempts to address the problem in the jurisdiction.

The steps to your review of jurisdictional conditions and potential solutions are these:

1. Once you have completed your SWOT Analysis, the next step is to review scholarly documents, reports, credible web-based material, for the establishment of a working annotative bibliography consisting of information about solutions discovered as useful for comparable jurisdictions that have attained success.
2. Conduct the research by decomposing the problem(s) confronting your jurisdiction. *See: Figure 2.1*
3. Organize the above information into subsets and record specific insights and strategies uncovered during your research.
4. To decompose the problem into subsets, you must know exactly what contributes to the presence of the problem and what

elements within the problem would have to change to either eliminate or minimize the severity of that problem for your jurisdiction. *Revisit: Figure 1.1*

5. Annotations should speak of successful strategies that have been used elsewhere to confront comparable circumstances.

6. You are to capture sufficient detail from your sources to inform your recommendations that will appear in your Action Plan.

7. In your search for what works, make sure you describe the successful processes, step by step, along with the skills and resources, along with the sequence of operation required.

8. Be prepared to give detailed instructions on how to implement the solution with diagrams included, if need be. The information must be sufficient to carry out your recommendation.

9. The length of each of your annotations will be dictated by the amount of detail you are able to glean on how to execute the strategy that has proven to work.

Assessing Priorities and Operational Linkages

Given the theoretical relation between collaborative action and outcomes for the community, obviously this requires criterion for acceptable performance. Success will depend on implementation of agreed upon collaborative responsibilities. Quality control of collective action comes from the monitoring of action in lined with established priorities and the configurative design for meeting those requirements. The goal then is to establish thresholds of acceptability and then implement collaborative learning strategies that build up operational capacity by covering the critical points required for community advancement.

As a consequence of such a vehicle for change means that the goal is served by the act of evidence collection alone. This thwarts actions that often absorb time, absorb attention, and absorb energy. Attributes that must be taken into consideration given collaborative efforts entail both within and between organizations:

1. Resource availability (i.e., staff configuration, staff scheduling, technology, expertise, funds, etc.)
2. Adequacy of information access to support decision-making for each division of operation (i.e., appropriateness of information made accessible);
3. Structural context in which the initiatives are made operative (i.e., complexity, requisites, gates, etc.);
4. Operational methods (i.e., staff requirements, utilization, efficiency of flow, timeliness of decisions, frequency of generation of information required for decision-making, number of decision rules, protocol for establishing decision rules, designated areas for independent judgment, number of delays, cost, rate of loss);
5. Operational structure (i.e., formal and informal organizational chart/communication patterns);
6. Lines of authority (i.e., decision points, decision rules);
7. Length of process associated with every activity/function
8. Degree of specificity of goals, objectives, sub-objectives, etc.

All of the above may be seen within the context of the following:

1. Characteristics of program component initiation and dissolution
2. Longevity of program components
3. Status of program components
4. Number of functions performed by program components
5. Diversity of functions performed within components
6. Conditions under which new components and/or functions are added
7. Number of consolidated components
8. Diversity of consolidated components
9. Characteristics of plans in relation to development
10. Point of consolidation (including the hub.)
11. Crosswalk between stated mission and implementation.
12. Plan of development in relation to political solvency factors

Chapter 7 – A Closing Note

The goal should be to help individuals to rise above subsistence and dependency, to attain the ability to give, and therefore do so. Configurative intervention should facilitate that process, offering protection while avoiding hindrances to progress. That which artificially promotes any action(s) to diminish an individual's ability to move forward with freedom, thus burdening rather than releasing the individual from the spirit of man-made dependency of any form, should be deemed counterproductive, no matter how much that effort is presumed as compassion in the minds of others.

EXERCISE 7 – MONITORING OUTCOMES

7.1 Identify the pertinent indicators for your chosen sector given your SWOT

7.2 Monitor change in Y using the most appropriate research strategy.

7.3 Organize data temporally or geographically by census tract in a manner most suited to the chosen applied research question(s) that if answered would be instrumental in improving quality of life in the jurisdiction.

SUGGESTED READING

Sector Indicators

Chandy, K. Mani, Brian Emre Aydemir, Elliott Michael Karpilosky and Daniel M. Zimmerman. "Event-Driven Architectures for Distributed Crisis Management." California Institute of Technology. Computer Science 256-80.

Drake, Alvin W., Ralph L. Keeney, and Philip M. Morse. *Analysis of Public Systems.* 1972.

International Conference on Vulnerability and Risk Analysis and Management, and Bilal M. Ayyub. *Vulnerability, Uncertainty, and Risk Analysis, Modeling and Management Proceedings of the First International Conference on Vulnerability and Risk Analysis and Management (ICVRAM 2011) and the Fifth International Symposium on Uncertainty Modeling and Analysis (ISUMA 2011)* : April 11-13, 2011, Hyattsville, Maryland. Reston, Va: American Society of Civil Engineers, 2011. <http://ascelibrary.org/isbn/978-0-7844-1170-4>.

Woodward, M. *Epidemiology: Study Design and Data Analysis.* Boca Raton: Chapman & Hall/CRC, 2005

Research Strategies

Achen, Christopher H. *The Statistical Analysis of Quasi-Experiments.* Berkeley: University of California Press, 1986.

Agresti, Alan. *Analysis of Ordinal Categorical Data.* New York: Wiley, 1984.

Collaborative Stewardship

Arnau Gras, Jaime. *Disen□ os Longitudinales Aplicados a Las Ciencias Sociales Y Del Comportamiento.* Me□ xico [etc.]: Limusa-Noriega, 1995

Baggaley, Andrew R. *Intermediate Correlational Methods.* New York: J. Wiley, 1964.

Boyd, Lawrence H., Jr. and Gudmund R. Iversen. 1979. *Contextual Analysis: Concepts and Statistical Techniques.* Belmont: Wadsworth Publishing Company.

Bradbury-Jones, Caroline, Julie Taylor, and Oliver Herber. 2014. "How Theory Is Used and Articulated in Qualitative Research: Development of a New Typology". *Social Science & Medicine.* 120: 135-141.

Fitz-Gibbon, Carol Taylor, and Lynn Lyons Morris. *How to Design a Program Evaluation. Beverly Hills, Calif: Sage Publications, 1978.*

Kish, Leslie. *Statistical Design for Research.* New York: Wiley, 1987.

Kanji, Gopal K. *100 Statistical tests.* Newbury Park, Calif. <etc.>: Sage, 1993.

Maddala, G. S. *Limited-Dependent and Qualitative Variables in Econometrics.* Cambridge [Cambridgeshire]: Cambridge University Press, 1983.

Manly, Bryan F. *The Design and Analysis of Research Studies.* New York: Cambridge University Press.1992.

Marascuilo, Leonard A., and Ronald C. Serlin. *Statistical Methods for the Social and Behavioral Sciences.* New York: W.H. Freeman, 1988.

Stinchcombe, Arthur L. *Constructing Social Theories.* Chicago: University of Chicago Press. 1987.

Applied Research Questions and Quality of Life

Bernard, H. Russell, et. al. 2001. "Estimating the Ripple Effect of a Disaster." *Connections,* 24(2): 30-34.

Box, George E. P., and George E. P. Box. *Improving Almost Anything: Ideas and Essays.* Hoboken, NJ: Wiley-Interscience, 2006.

Bruning, James L., and B. L. Kintz. *Computational Handbook of Statistics.* New York, NY [u.a.]: Longman, 1999.

Evans, James R., and David Louis Olson. Statistics, Data Analysis, and Decision Modeling. Upper Saddle River, NJ: Prentice Hall, 2000.

Lempert, Robert J., Steven W. Popper, Steen C. Bankes.. Shaping the Next One Hundred Years: New Methods for Quantitative, Long-Term Policy Analysis. Santa Monica: Rand. 2003.

Mohr, Lawrence B. *Impact Analysis for Program Evaluation.* Thousand Oaks, Calif: Sage Publications, 1995.

Parnell, Gregory S., Parnell, Terry Bresnick, MBA., and S. Tani. *Handbook of Decision Analysis.* John Wiley & Sons, 2013.

Przeworski, Adam, and Henry Teune. *The Logic of Comparative Social Inquiry.* New York: Wiley-Interscience, 1970.

Scholz, Roland W., and Olaf Tietje. *Embedded Case Study Methods: Integrating Quantitative and Qualitative Knowledge.* Thousand Oaks, Calif: Sage Publications, 2002.

Vose, David. *Risk analysis: a quantitative guide.* Chichester [u.a.]: Wiley, 2010.

Yin, Robert K. *Applications of Case Study Research.* Thousand Oaks: Sage Publications. 2003.

Yin, Robert K. *Case Study Research: Design and Methods.* Thousand Oaks: Sage Publications. 2003.

8

CHANGING IMPACT

"For you will spread out to the right and the left, your descendants will possess the nations and inhabit the desolated cities."
---Isaiah 54: 2, *Holy Bible*, CJB

-

Determining Focus. Determining Corrective Action. Changing Operational Linkages. Measuring Progress.

Figure 8.1 - System of Systems – Common Operating Picture for Sequential Response

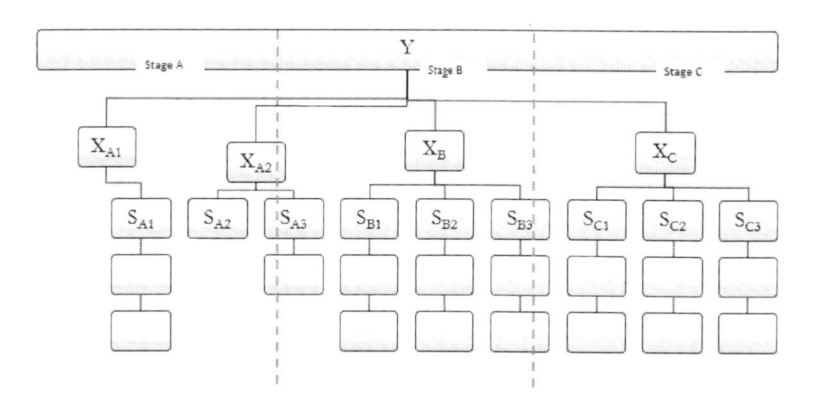

Indicators of success require specification. Definitive statements of how we will know when we have arrived means that activity will be endorsed, squelching ambiguity and hidden agendas, thus affording activities that support civic purposes. Related to indicators of success is the issue of threshold establishing a point of comparison between what is and what would have been had no intervention taken place. This notion can be expressed as a simple coefficient of effectiveness or as elaborately as the use of the evaluation estimation equations

We Must Identify Challenges and Then Look for Potential Solutions, not the Reverse!

Consider,

Responding to Constraint #1:

- Varied nature of organizations serving the jurisdiction

Solution: Craft "tailor-made" correspondence for select organizations/and organizational configurations

Responding to Constraint #2:

- Varied perspectives on problem definition

Solution: Generate collaborative opportunities to redefine problems, scrutinizing the merits of the definition explored, and collaboratively communicating through bulleted summaries

Responding to Constraint #3:

- Varied definitions of progress[30]

Solution: State values and then express those in concrete terms as alternate measures of progress, making explicit thresholds of acceptability.

Responding to Constraint #4:

---

[30] See: Ralph L Keeney and Howard Raiffa. *Decisions with Multiple Objectives: Preferences and Value Tradeoffs.* New York: Wiley, 1976.

- Varied political affiliation and covering

Solution: Orchestrate collective learning about the impact of roles across the Organizational Network Configuration

Responding to Constraint #5:

- Overarching cultural and/or linguistic affiliation

Solution: Find common ground on issues directly, measurably, related to quality of life in the jurisdiction

Responding to Constraint #6:

- Domestic counterbalances such that ethnic/racial/religious affiliation/ attachment that may supersede concern for the community-at-large

Solution: Leverage these in a way that expresses tangible benefit for all residents.

Responding to Constraint #7:

- Geopolitical considerations in defining shared threat, benefit, future

Solution: Release statements directed toward select clusters behind which all may agree due to the nature of how the threat is explained.

Responding to Constraint #8:

- Vacillation or vacuum inadvertently caused by the absence of coherent mission statement or the presence of a contradictory definition of mission must be countered or otherwise avoided effectively

Solution: Offer alternative, a God-honoring, interpretation of events that focus on aspects supportive of progress

Responding to Constraint #9:

Collaborative Stewardship

- Priority among stakeholders identified on the basis of monetary and political constraints

Solution: Establish a new context.

Measuring Impact

With regard to the summative "impact" the collaborative activity on the community, the issue of expected versus actual outcomes requires a panoramic review of action. Institutions become a frame of reference for the discussion of policy recommendations and choices, thus answering the question: What difference did collective intervention make for the community? The goal is to strategically communicate options based upon thorough research of best practices and then pursue relevant action collectively to secure improved quality of life.

Having an audience for the results is important because evaluations are to be used. And, the determination of usefulness rests on how the audience (often referred to as stakeholders) perceives value. Not all who may be affected may be deemed stakeholders. For political response, persons that may benefit may have been excluded from policy/programmatic conversation.

CHANGING OPERATIONAL LINKAGES

The organizational arrangements/network-wide configuration for the jurisdiction must be seen as offering a credible gain to stakeholders; i.e., preventing loss of that which is seen as of value to stakeholders.

Figure 8.2 Fault Tree Schematic for Accountability, Discrepancy and Change

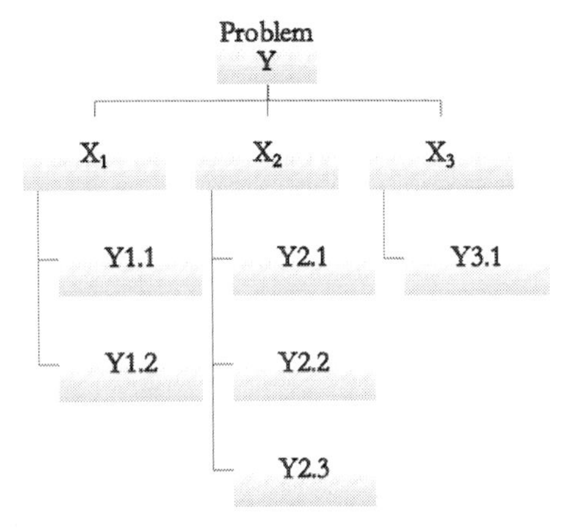

$Y_1 + \ldots + Y_N =$ Component Functions required to operate if Y is to become a desired outcome.

Collaborative Stewardship

The message must accomplish the following:

- Recognize tangible [quantifiable] evidence of benefit gleaned by current and emerging structure
- Recognize action points as required for continuation
- Be able to gauge the cost/benefit ratio of the contribution of each individual organization to the collective configuration
- See evidence of configurative information exchange improving operation
- Become vested in the mission
- See shared action on declared priorities yield results
- And, perceive credibility, integrity, and accountability of operations

Counterfactual—what would be if we did nothing; or, better put, what would be the consequence of the absence of any linkages within a network.

Another essential element is to determine whether an initiative can be evaluated. The yardstick for determining "evaluability" of an initiative is as follows:

1. Implementation according to design has been accomplished;
2. Data exists or can be generated on performance;
3. There is a standard for comparison
4. Some one really wants to know about performance

The element of having sufficient information is nontrivial. It also precludes the following problems:

1. Too much information to make a judgment;
2. Information generation, where research is used as a stall technique;
3. Irrelevant information;
4. Timeliness;
5. Access where appropriate, determined on the basis of information flow, planning, and evaluation efforts.

Conclusion of the Matter: Measuring Impact

The message is this: We should steward our communities collaboratively and do so following the example of our Creator, approaching the work according to "intelligent" design.

Assessment of expected versus actual outcomes really does require a panoramic review of directed action, logically prescribed to meet needs. Rather than limiting the focus to linkages between individuals and entities, focus should be on functions to be performed and the arrangement that maximizes the likelihood of desirable outcome for the community. The conversation must not be limited to planning circles as options best suited for a jurisdiction may not follow traditional patterns as if one size of fits all. Broadening the frame of reference for the discussion of policy recommendations and choices may promote answers previously overlooked. Asking the question, "*What difference collectively does intervention make for the community?*" is an essential step toward effective collaborative stewardship if we wish to improve the quality of life for our communities.

Chapter 8 – A Closing Note

Functions performed must conform to God's description of the human condition as expressed in the Holy Bible. God grants talents. Every effort should be made to identify the calling of not only organizations but individuals in order to identify the specific function each is called to perform within the context God has placed them. Vulnerabilities may be ongoing or come as a result of some cataclysmic event. The approach for addressing those vulnerabilities is the same. It is only the point of emphasis and scope that may differ. *See Postscript.*

SUGGESTED READING

Edwards, Ward, and J. Robert Newman. *Multiattribute Evaluation*. Newbury Park, Calif. [u.a.]: Sage, 1993

Keeney, Ralph L. "Foundations for Group Decision Analysis." *Decision Analysis* 10, no.2 (2013): 103-20. http://dx.doi.org/doi:10.1287/deca.2013.0265.

Keeney, Ralph L. *Value-Focused Thinking: A Path to Creative Decision-making.* Cambridge, Mass: Harvard University Press, 1992.

Kirsh, David. 2006. "Methodologies for Evaluating Collaboration Behavior in Co-Located Environments." kirsh@ucsd.edu.

POSTSCRIPT

God's written word, the *Holy Bible*, is true and it is relevant to all aspects of life including the active pursuit of improved quality of life in community.

I find it quite interesting that in the biblical Hebrew the word for "Life" is the same word used for "Community," pronounced *Chai*. God is the Creator of Life, thus as good stewards we should pursue preservation of Life. We do this in honor of the Author of Life, God. Success is to know and then act on the written word of God. One of the passages that appearing especially relevant to our pursuit of improved quality of life in community is Proverbs 22: 2-4, the Holy Bible, KJV. It reads:

"Rich and poor have this in common: The Lord is the maker of them all."

*

"A prudent man sees danger and takes refuge, but the simple keep going and suffer for it."

*

"Humility and the fear of the Lord bring wealth and honor and life."

In my book entitled, *Acknowledging God in the Decisions of State: A Treatise on Biblically-Informed Statesmanship*, 2nd *Edition*[31], I expressed my interest in all aspects of

---

[31] See McDonald, Olivia M. McDonald, *Acknowledging God in the Decisions of State: A Treatise on Biblically-Informed Statesmanship.* 2nd Ed. Suffolk, VA: Grace House Publishing, 2015.

organization, especially in that of establishing order. Prayerfully approaching that question during my Bible study, I discovered the scriptural address to solution in Chapter 1 of Genesis. That first chapter of the Holy Bible discusses the sequence God used to create order out of chaos. For your convenience, I have reproduced an excerpt from my 2nd edition work. You will be able to see the roots of my thought process aligned to the actual Bible verses. Such correspondence of ideas underlies the *Collaborative Stewardship* approach in this book.

Because maladies confronting jurisdictions are ongoing and include susceptibility to natural and man-made disaster, we must be cognizant of the fact that the *"birth pains"* Christ Jesus speaks of in the books of Matthew, Mark, and Luke are on God's schedule to increase in both frequency and intensity. Our active response, so that we may provide *Salt* and *Light* to those situations, should bear witness to God's goodness even in the midst of trouble. Consequently, I urge you to consider what appears below. Once you understand how the overall strategy aligns with the written word of God, the *Holy Bible*, I urge you to revisit the three stages I have outlined in this current work. Use a biblical lens and view the three-stage process of Accountability, Discrepancy, and Change. And, of course, when exercising collaborative stewardship, I am confident that we will do so to the honor and glory of God in Christ Jesus. Amen!

Consider the following approach:

#1---*Recognize God as Creator, the Source of origin*

#2---*Recognize the actual state of affairs, all of its important attributes, along with the tools God has made available to address the issues at hand.*

#3---*Execute actions that support visibility, the ability to see things as they really are*

#4---*Determine whether or not that which is used to make visible the status is good, valid, reliable, reflective of the* TRUTH. *And, if it is good, separate that which enables visibility from that which obscures or otherwise inhibits the needed visibility.*

#5---*Label the difference*

#6---*Be cognizant of time in relation to the tool of visibility*

#7---*Sort, differentiating with relevant precision------not just lumping like things together, but identifying relevant differences and sorting accordingly.*

#8---*Create a means of separating the differentiated elements.*

#9---*Come to completion on differentiation. Label while remaining cognizant of your use of time.*

#10---*Put like items in a shared location different from other things.*

#11---*Come to completion on placement.*

#12---*Label*

#13---*Assess what you have done so far.*

#14---*Take what you have and set up conditions for fruitful production (functions that produce desired outcomes), meaning identify that which has within itself all that is needed to reproduce, and organize that production according to its kind.*

#15---*Assess how you have set up the conditions in which production is to take place*

#16---*Determine whether there is a right match between what is to be produced where and the kind of yield expected.*

#17---*Look at this initiative in context to determine whether or not it is good.*

#18---*Be cognizant of time. Mark it.*

#20---*Apply the yardstick of visibility as the gauge for assessing categories of actions, routines, operation of productivity over time.*

#21---*Come to completion in the development of that gauge.*

#22---*Develop signals differencing stages of the work: stages of high visibility and low visibility.*

#23---*Develop elementary indicators to monitor during periods of low visibility.*

#24---*Use indicators*

#25---*Assess those indicators and remain cognizant of time. Mark it.*

#26---*Populate with that which is best suited for the environment/ structure/ operation you have created.*

#27---*Populate according to kind.*

#28---*Assess population fit.*

#29---*Establish conditions favorable for reproducibility according to kind in the first structures you created.*

#30---*Remain cognizant of time. Mark it.*

#31---*Establish conditions conducive to reproduction according to kind in the secondary structures produced.*

#32---*Come to completion on initiating populations.*

#33--- *Make sure initiated populations are according to kind.*

#34--- *Assess the populating process.*

#35--- *Mentor or apprentice folks you have prayerfully chosen, of like mind to yourself, and teach them all you know.*

#36--- *Recognize the different roles and capabilities of those you have mentored.*

#37--- *Put apprentices in positions to be productive applying what they have learned, and let them reproduce the process replicating themselves.*

#38--- *Give your apprentices charge over specific populations.*

#39--- *Instruct apprentices on how to become self---sustaining given all that was created.*

#40--- *Recognize and communicate what is consumable for sustainment.*

#41---*Identify all assets available to sustain those you have given charge.*

#42--- *Come to completion on this.*

#43--- *Assess the entire operation.*

Appendix: Excerpt from Acknowledging God in the Decisions of State, 2nd

ACTION POINT[32]

Finding the Scriptural Address of the Problem

Of course, study the Word of God to understand who we are and who God has equipped us to be. But, also, test every idea on the basis of the Bible. Jesus Christ said of Himself, *"I only do the things I see My Father doing."* John 5:19, *Holy Bible*. I believe that is what we need to do, too! It behooves us to prayerfully consult the Holy Bible to find the scriptural address of the topic of interest. In my case, I am interested in exploring elements associated with correcting organizational activity. Here is how I approached the question during my study of the Holy Bible. I found the scriptural address to be Chapter 1 of Genesis. That passage discusses God creating order out of chaos. Consider the following:

When we read Chapters 1 of Genesis we find a pattern of making order out of chaos.
For your convenience, Chapter 1 is presented here.
"In the beginning God created the heavens and the earth.
#1-[*Recognition of God as Creator, the Source of origin*]

Now the earth was formless and empty, darkness was over the surface of the deep, and the Spirit of God was hovering over the waters.
#2-[*Recognition of the actual state of affairs, all of its important attributes, along with the tools God has made available to address the issues at hand.*]

And God said, 'Let there be light,' and there was light.
#3-[*Execute actions that support visibility, the ability to see things as they really are*]
REMEMBER: "The word of God is a lamp unto our feet and a light unto our path."
All ideas/proposals must rightly align with what is written in the Holy Bible, Saints.

[32] *Ibid, p. 91-95*

God saw that the light was good, and he separated the light from the darkness.
#4-[*Determine whether or not that which is used to make visible the status is good, valid, reliable, that which reflective of the TRUTH. And, if it is good, separate that which enables visibility from that which obscures or otherwise inhibits the needed visibility.*]

God called the light 'day,' and the darkness he called 'night.'
#5-[*Label the difference*]

And, there was evening, and there was morning—the first day.
#6-[*Be cognizant of time in relation to the tool of visibility*]

And God said, 'Let there be a vault between the waters to separate water from water.'

#7-[*Sort, differentiating with relevant precision--not just lumping like things together, but identifying relevant differences and sorting accordingly.*]

So, God made the vault and separated the water under the vault from the water above it.
#8-[*Create a means of separating the differentiated elements.*]

And it was so.
#9-[*Come to completion on differentiation*]

God called the vault 'sky.' And there was evening, and there was morning—the second day.
[*Label while remaining cognizant of your use of time.*]

And God said, 'Let the water under the sky be gathered to one place, and let dry ground appear.'
#10-[*Put like items in a shared location different from other things.*]

And it was so.
#11-[*Come to completion on placement.*]

God called the dry ground 'land,' and the gathered waters he called 'seas.'
#12-[*Label*]

And God saw that it was good.
#13-[*Assess what you have done so far.*]

Then God said, 'Let the land produce vegetation: seed-bearing plants and trees on the land that bear fruit with seed in it, according to their various kinds.'
#14-[*Take what you have and set up conditions for fruitful production, meaning identify that which has within itself all that is needed to reproduce, and organize that production according to its kind.*]

And it was so.

#15-[*Assess how you have set up the conditions in which production is to take place*]

The land produced vegetation: plants bearing seed according
to their kinds and trees bearing fruit with seed in it according
to their kinds.
#16-[*Determine whether there is a right match between what is to be produced where and the kind of yield expected.*]

And God saw that it was good.
#17-[*Look at this initiative in context to determine whether or not it is good.*]
And there was evening, and there was morning—the third day.
#18-[*Be cognizant of time. Mark it.*]

And God said, 'Let there be lights in the vault of the sky to separate the day from the night, and let them serve as signs to mark sacred times, and days and years, and let them be lights in the vault of the sky to give light on the earth.'
#20-[*Apply the yardstick of visibility as the gauge for assessing categories of actions, routines, operation of productivity over time.*]

And it was so.
#21-[*Come to completion in the development of that gauge.*]

God made two great lights—the greater light to govern the day and the lesser light to govern the night.
#22-[*Develop signals differencing stages of the work: stages of high visibility and low visibility.*]

He also made the stars.
#23-[*Develop elementary indicators to monitor during periods of low visibility.*]

God set them in the vault of the sky to give light on the earth, to govern the day and the night, and to separate light from darkness.
#24-[*Use indicators*]

And God saw that it was good. And there was evening, and there was morning—the fourth day.
#25-[*Assess those indicators and remain cognizant of time. Mark it.*]

And God said, 'Let the water teem with living creatures, and let birds fly above the earth across the vault of the sky.'
#26-[*Populate with that which is best suited for the environment/structure/operation you have created.*]

So God created the great creatures of the sea and every living thing with which the water teems and that moves about in it, according to their kinds, and every winged bird according to its kind.

#27-[*Populate according to kind.*]

And God saw that it was good.
#28-[*Assess population fit.*]

God blessed them and said, 'Be fruitful and increase in number and fill the water in the seas, and let the birds increase on the earth.'
#29-[*Establish conditions favorable for reproducibility according to kind in the first structures you created*].

And there was evening, and there was morning—the fifth day.
#30-[*Remain cognizant of time. Mark it.*]

And God said,'Let the land produce living creatures according to their kinds: the livestock, the creatures that move along the ground, and the wild animals, each according to its kind.'
#31-[*Establish conditions conducive to reproduction according to kind in the secondary structures produced.*]

And it was so.
#32-[*Come to completion on initiating populations.*]

God made the wild animals according to their kinds, the livestock according to their kinds, and all the creatures that move along the ground according to their kinds.
#33-[*Make sure initiated populations are according to kind.*]

And God saw that it was good.
#34-[*Assess the populating process.*]

Then God said, 'Let us make mankind in our image, in our likeness, so that they may rule over the fish in the sea and the birds in the sky, over the livestock and all the wild animals, and over all the creatures that move along the ground.'
#35-[*Mentor or apprentice folks you have prayerfully chosen, of like mind to yourself, and teach them all you know.*]

So God created mankind in his own image, in the image of God he created them; male and female he created them.
#36-[*Recognize the different roles and capabilities of those you have mentored.*]

God blessed them and said to them, "Be fruitful and increase in number; fill the earth and subdue it.
#37-[*Put apprentices in positions to be productive applying what they have learned, and let them reproduce the process replicating themselves.*]

Rule over the fish in the sea and the birds in the sky and over every living creature that moves on the ground.'
#38-[*Give your apprentices charge over specific populations.*]

Then God said, 'I give you every seed-bearing plant on the face of the whole earth and every tree that has fruit with seed in it.
#39- [*Instruct apprentices on how to become self-sustaining given all that was created.]*

They will be yours for food.
#40-[*Recognize and communicate what is consumable for sustainment.*]

And to all the beasts of the earth and all the birds in the sky and all the creatures that move along the ground—everything that has the breath of life in it—I give every green plant for food.'
#41-[*Identify all assets available to sustain those you have given charge.]*

And it was so.
#42-[*Come to completion on this*]

God saw all that he had made, and it was very good. And there was evening, and there was morning — the sixth day."
#43-[*Assess the entire operation.*]

The above constitute the steps I have prayerfully derived from reading Genesis 1 of the Holy Bible. In that Bible passage we see that God took that which was out of order and created that which would be fruitful by design. Let us do likewise in the spheres of influence God has assigned us. Let us be productive in our work by first rightly ordering our soul by rightly acknowledging God in every aspect of our life. And, as we do so, God can direct our steps as we govern to His glory.

Please check all that has been written here on the basis of Holy Scripture.[33]

---

[33]There are many Bible-Believing Scientists I could point to so that you may know that prayerfully consulting the Holy Bible is not new to the scientific community. However, I have chosen just one. If you wish more examples, I recommend that you read the book entitled, *Biblical Basis for Modern Science*, by Henry M. Morris (Green Forest, AR: Master Books, 2002). For now, I invite you to consider **Louis Pasteur**, the father of ***"pasteurization,"*** in response to his prayerful study of the written Word of God in attempt to discover what was causing the onslaught of disease in a community, had his eyes land on the following verse: "Through faith we understand that the worlds were framed by the word of God, so that things which are seen were not made of things which do appear." Hebrews 11:3 KJV "That which is invisible comes from that which is invisible." Hebrews 11:3 [*My Paraphrase*] Do Note: Pasteur did not use that singular verse as a "tag-along" to his own thin collection of thoughts. No, He started with that verse as the driving force behind his research. Accepting the entire Holy Bible as true, relevant, worth acting on, Pasteur proceeded to devise his research agenda based on Truth. Pasteur decided to dig deeply into the truthfulness of that statement found in the written word of God, the Holy Bible! As an extension of that Biblical understanding, Pasteur decided that it may be necessary to rid impurities from food substances, impurities that are not detectable with the "naked eye." From the reasoning process consistent with the written Word of God and no doubt guided by the Presence of the Holy Spirit, Pasteur arrives at what we now refer to as "Germ" Theory, thus saving millions of lives from that biblically-based insight. He took that Bible Truth and then actively searched out/investigated. His study resulted in fruitfulness. Here is Pasteur's account in his own words: "Blessed is he who carries within himself God and an ideal and who obeys it — an ideal of art, of science, or Gospel virtues. Therein lie the springs of great thoughts and great actions; they all reflect light from the Infinite. (*The Wordsworth Dictionary of Quotations*, 1998 by Connie Robertson, p. 320)

God Speed!
---Olivia M. McDonald

REFERENCES

Aarons, Gregory A., Michael Hurlburt, and Sarah McCue Horwitz. 2011. "Advancing a Conceptual Model of Evidence-Based Practice Implementation in Public Service Sectors". *Administration and Policy in Mental Health and Mental Health Services Research.* 38, no. 1: 4-23.

Achen, Christopher H. *The Statistical Analysis of Quasi-Experiments.* Berkeley: University of California Press, 1986.

Acosta, Joie, Stefanie Howard, Anita Chandra, Danielle M. Varda, Sara Sprong, and Lori Uscher-Pines. 2015. "Contributions of Health Care Coalitions to Preparedness and Resilience: Perspectives from Hospital Preparedness Program and Health Care Preparedness Coalitions". *Disaster Medicine and Public Health Preparedness.*

Agresti, Alan. *Analysis of Ordinal Categorical Data.* New York: Wiley, 1984.

Arnau Gras, Jaime. *Disen□ os Longitudinales Aplicados a Las Ciencias Sociales Y Del Comportamiento.* Me□ xico [etc.]: Limusa-Noriega, 1995

Axelrod, Robert M. *The Structure of Decision: The Cognitive Maps of Political Elites.* 1977.

Baggaley, Andrew R. *Intermediate Correlational Methods.* New York: J. Wiley, 1964.

Ben-Haim, Yakov. *Info-Gap Economics: An Operational Introduction.* Basingstoke [England]: Palgrave Macmillan, 2010.

Ben-Haim, Yakov, and Yakov Ben-Haim. *Info-Gap Decision Theory: Decisions Under Severe Uncertainty.* Oxford: Academic, 2006. <http://site.ebrary.com/id/10151385>.

Ben-Haim, Yakov. *Info-Gap Robust-Satisficing and the Probability of Survival.* 2007.

Berke, Philip R., Jack D. Kartez, and Dennis Wenger. *Recovery After Disaster: Achieving Sustainable Development, Mitigation and Equity*. 1993.

Bernard, H. Russell, et. al. 2001. "Estimating the Ripple Effect of a Disaster." *Connections,* 24(2): 30-34.

Box, George E. P., and George E. P. Box. *Improving Almost Anything: Ideas and Essays*. Hoboken, NJ: Wiley-Interscience, 2006.

Boyd, Lawrence H., Jr. and Gudmund R. Iversen. 1979. *Contextual Analysis: Concepts and Statistical Techniques*. Belmont: Wadsworth Publishing Company.

Bradbury-Jones, Caroline, Julie Taylor, and Oliver Herber. 2014. "How Theory Is Used and Articulated in Qualitative Research: Development of a New Typology". *Social Science & Medicine.* 120: 135-141.

Bruning, James L., and B. L. Kintz. *Computational Handbook of Statistics*. New York, NY [u.a.]: Longman, 1999.

Burkle, Frederick M. 2001. "The Concept of Assisted Management of Large-Scale Disasters by Horizontal Organizations." http://pdm.medicine.wisc.edu.

Burt, Ronald S., and Michael J. Minor. *Applied Network Analysis: A Methodological Introduction*. Beverly Hills: Sage Publications, 1983.

Canary H.E., Ghorbani S.S., and Blevins M. 2014. "Organizational Policy Communication Research: Challenges, Discoveries, and Future Directions". *Communication Reports.*

Carley, Kathleen M. et. al. 2002. "Destabilizing Networks." *Connections* 24(3): 79-92.

Castells, Manuel. *The Rise of the Network Society*. Malden: Blackwell Publishers. 2000.

Cawson, Alan. *Corporatism and Political Theory*. New York: Basil Blackwell Inc. 1986.

Chandy, K. Mani, Brian Emre Aydemir, Elliott Michael Karpilosky and Daniel M. Zimmerman. "Event-Driven Architectures for Distributed Crisis Management." California Institute of Technology. Computer Science 256-80.

Chen, Huey-tsyh. *Practical Program Evaluation: Assessing and Improving Planning,*

Implementation, and Effectiveness. Thousand Oaks, Calif: Sage, 2005. <http://public.eblib.com/choice/publicfullrecord.aspx?p=3032344>.

Chen, Huey-tsyh. *Theory-Driven Evaluations*. Newbury Park, Calif: Sage Publications, 1990.

Chen, Huey-tsyh, and Peter H. Rossi. *Using Theory to Improve Program and Policy Evaluations*. New York: Greenwood Press, 1992.

Clemen, Robert T. *Making Hard Decisions: An Introduction*. [Pacific Grove, CA]: Duxbury Press, 1996.

Cliquennois G. 2013. "Which Penology for Decision Making in French Prisons?" *Punishment and Society*. 15, no. 5: 468-487.

Coleman, James S. *Foundations of Social Theory*. Cambridge, Mass: Belknap Press of Harvard University Press, 1990.

Creswell, John W. *Research Design: Qualitative, Quantitative, and Mixed Method Approaches*. Thousand Oaks, Calif: Sage Publications, 2003.

Cross, Jennifer Eileen, Ellyn Dickmann, Rebecca Newman-Gonchar, and Jesse Michael Fagan. 2009. "Using Mixed-Method Design and Network Analysis to Measure Development of Interagency Collaboration". *American Journal of Evaluation*. 30, no. 3: 310-329.

Cutter, Susan L., Lindsey Barnes, Melissa Berry, Christopher Burton, Elijah Evans, Eric Tate, and Jennifer Webb. 2008. "A Place-Based Model for Understanding Community Resilience to Natural Disasters". Global Environmental Change. 18, no. 4: 598-606.

Dao, Hy and Pascal Peduzzi. 2004. "Global Evaluation of Human Risk and Vulnerability to Natural Hazards." Enviro-info, Sh@ring, Editions du Tricorne, Geneva, Vol. 1:435-446.

DECISIONS AND DESIGNS INC MCLEAN VA, Fischhoff, Baruch, Slovic, Paul, and Lichtenstein, Sarah. *Fault Trees: Sensitivity of Estimated Failure Probabilities to Problem Representation*\. 1977.
<http://oai.dtic.mil/oai/oai?&verb=getRecord&metadataPrefix=html&identifier=

ADA057163>.

Drake, Alvin W., Ralph L. Keeney, and Philip M. Morse. *Analysis of Public Systems.* 1972.

Durand, Roger, Phillip J. Decker, and Dorothy M. Kirkman. 2014. "Evaluation Methodologies for Estimating the Likelihood of Program Implementation Failure".*American Journal of Evaluation.* 35, no. 3: 404-418.

Earl, Sarah, F. Carden, Michael Quinn Patton, and Terry Smutylo. *Outcome Mapping Building Learning and Reflection into Development Programs*. Ottawa: International Development Research Centre, 2001. <http://www.deslibris.ca/ID/405863>.

Edwards, Ward, and J. Robert Newman. *Multiattribute Evaluation*. Newbury Park, Calif. [u.a.]: Sage Publ, 1993.

Eisenberg M, and N Swanson. 1996. "Organizational Network Analysis as a Tool for Program Evaluation". *Evaluation & the Health Professions.* 19, no. 4: 488-506.

Evans, James R., and David Louis Olson. Statistics, Data Analysis, and Decision Modeling. Upper Saddle River, NJ: Prentice Hall, 2000.

Fischhoff, Baruch. *Judgment and Decision Making*. Abingdon Oxon: Earthscan, 2012.

Freeman, Linton C., and Douglas R. White. *Research Methods in Social Network Analysis.* New Brunswick, NJ <etc.>: Transaction Publishers, 1992.

Fleury, Marie-Jose□ e, Grenier, Guy, Lesage, Alain, Ma, Nan, and Ngui, Andre□ Ngamini.*Network Collaboration of Organisations for Homeless Individuals in the Montreal Region*. Igitur publishing, 2014.
<http://www.ncbi.nlm.nih.gov/pmc/articles/PMC3920820>.

Flom, Peter L. et. al. 2004. "A New Measure of Linkage Between Two Sub-Networks." *Connections*, 26(1): 62-70.

Fitz-Gibbon, Carol Taylor, and Lynn Lyons Morris. *How to Design a Program Evaluation. Beverly Hills, Calif: Sage Publications, 1978.*

Funnell, S. C. *2000. "Developing and Using a Program Theory Matrix for Program Evaluation and Performance Monitoring". NEW DIRECTIONS FOR EVALUATION. no. 87: 91-102.*

Galport, N., and T. Azzam. 2016. "Evaluator Training Needs and Competencies: A Gap Analysis". *American Journal of Evaluation.*

Gates, E., and L. Dyson. 2016. "Implications of the Changing Conversation About Causality for Evaluators". *American Journal of Evaluation.*

Gill, Jeff. *Bayesian Methods A Social and Behavioral Sciences Approach.* Bayesian Methods. Boca Raton, FL: CRC Press, Taylor & Francis Group, 2015.

Green, Gary P., and Anna Haines. *Asset Building & Community Development.* 2016.

Hammond, Kenneth R. and American Association for the Advancement of Science. *Judgment and Decision in Public Policy Formation.* AAAS Selected Symposium 1. Boulder, Colo.: Published by Westview Press for the American Association for the Advancement of Science, 1978.

Hanneman, Robert A. and Mark Riddle. *Introduction to social network methods.* Riverside, CA: University of California, Riverside.2005. (Published in digital form at http://faculty.ucr.edu/~hanneman/)

Hidalgo-Hardeman, Olivia M. A *Probabilistic Analysis of Social Services Network Failure.* Corpus Christi: Coastal Bend Council of Governments. 1988.

Hidalgo-Hardeman, Olivia M. 1993. "Evaluating Social Service Delivery Configurations."*Evaluation Review.* 17, no. 6: 603-20.

Hogwood, Brian W., and Brainard Guy Peters. *The Pathology of Public Policy:* Oxford: Clarendon Pr, 1985.

Honeycutt, Todd C., and Debra A. Strong. 2012. "Using Social Network Analysis to Predict Early Collaboration Within Health Advocacy Coalitions". *American Journal of Evaluation.* 33, no. 2: 221-239.

Huisman, Mark, and Marijtje A.J. van Duijn Software for Social Network Analysis. Heymans Institute/DPMG and Statistics & Measurement Theory, University of

Groningen,3rd October 2003.
http://stat.gamma.rug.nl/snijders/Software%20for%20Social%20Network%20Analysis%20CUP_ch13_Oct2003.pdf for a convenient summary of SNA related software.

International Conference on Vulnerability and Risk Analysis and Management, and Bilal M. Ayyub. *Vulnerability, Uncertainty, and Risk Analysis, Modeling and Management Proceedings of the First International Conference on Vulnerability and Risk Analysis and Management (ICVRAM 2011) and the Fifth International Symposium on Uncertainty Modeling and Analysis (ISUMA 2011)* : April 11-13, 2011, Hyattsville, Maryland. Reston, Va: American Society of Civil Engineers, 2011. <http://ascelibrary.org/isbn/978-0-7844-1170-4>.

International Economic Development Council - Disaster_Recovery_Webinar_Series
http://www.iedconline.org/web-pages/conferences-events/2015-disaster-preparedness-recovery-series/

Ishikawa, Kaoru. *Guide to Quality Control.* Tokyo: Asian Productivity Organization, 1986.

Judd, Charles M., and David kenny. *Estimating the Effects of Social Interventions.* Cambridge, [etc]: Cambridge University press, 1981.

Kapuchu, Naim. 2005. "Interorganizational Coordination in Dynamic Context: Networks in Emergency Response Management." Connections, 26(2): 33-48.

Katzer, Jeffrey, Kenneth H. Cook, and Wayne W. Crouch. *Evaluating Information: A Guide for Users of Social Science Research.* Boston, Mass: McGraw-Hill, 1998.

Kavoura, Androniki, and Evgenia Bitsani. 2014. "Methodological Considerations for Qualitative Communication Research". *Procedia - Social and Behavioral Sciences.* 147: 544-549.

Keeney, Ralph L. "Structuring Objectives for Problems of Public Interest." *Operations Research* 36, no. 3 (1988): 396-405.
http://dx.doi.org/doi:10.1287/opre.36.3.396.

Keeney, Ralph L. *Value-Focused Thinking: A Path to Creative Decision making.* Cambridge, Mass.: Harvard University Press, 1992.

Keeney, Ralph L. "Value-Focused Brainstorming." *Decision Analysis* 9, no. 4 (2012): 303-13. http://dx.doi.org/10.1287/deca.1120.0251.

Keeney, Ralph L. "Foundations for Group Decision Analysis." *Decision Analysis* 10, no.2 (2013): 103-20. http://dx.doi.org/doi:10.1287/deca.2013.0265.

Keeney Ralph L. 1970. "Assessment of Multi-Attribute Preferences". *Science (New York, N.Y.)*. 168, no. 3938: 1491-2.

Keeney, Ralph L., and Howard Raiffa. *Decisions with Multiple Objectives: Preferences and Value Tradeoffs*. New York: Wiley, 1976.

Kirsh, David. 2006. "Methodologies for Evaluating Collaboration Behavior in Co-Located Environments." kirsh@ucsd.edu.

Kish, Leslie. *Statistical Design for Research*. New York: Wiley, 1987.

Knoke, David, and James H. Kuklinski. *Network Analysis*. Newbury Park, Calif. [u.a.]: Sage Publ, 2002.

Kume, Hitoshi. *Statistical Methods for Quality Improvement*. Tokyo: Association for Overseas Technical Scholarship, 1985.

Kanji, Gopal K. *100 Statistical tests*. Newbury Park, Calif. <etc.>: Sage, 1993.

Langley, Pat. *Elements of Machine Learning*. San Francisco, Calif: Morgan Kaufmann, 1996.

Laumann, Edward O., and David Knoke. *The Organizational State: Social Choice in National Policy Domains*. Madison, Wis: University of Wisconsin Press, 1987.

Leigh, Nancey Green, and Edward J. Blakely. *Planning Local Economic Development: Theory and Practice*. 2013.

Leinhardt, Samuel. *Social Networks*. Elsevier Science, 2013. <http://lib.myilibrary.com?id=665144>.

Lempert, Robert J., Steven W. Popper, Steen C. Bankes.. Shaping the Next One Hundred Years: New Methods for Quantitative, Long-Term Policy Analysis. Santa Monica: Rand. 2003.

Lewis, Darrell R., David R. Johnson, and Troy Mangen. 1998. "Evaluating the Multidimensional Nature of Supported Employment[1]". *Journal of Applied Research in Intellectual Disabilities.* 11, no. 2: 95-115.

Lin, Nan. *Foundations of Social Research.* New York: McGraw-Hill, 1976. Mahnič, Nika. 2014. "Gamification of Politics: Start a New Game!" *Teorija in Praksa.* no. 51.

Løkketangen, Arne, Johan Oppen, Jorge Oyola, and David Woodruff. 2012. "An Attribute Based Similarity Function for VRP Decision Support". *Decision Making in Manufacturing and Services.* 6, no. 2: 65.

Maddala, G. S. *Limited-Dependent and Qualitative Variables in Econometrics.* Cambridge [Cambridgeshire]: Cambridge University Press, 1983.

Malmberg, Anders, and Peter Maskell. *Localized Learning Revisited.* 2005.

Manly, Bryan F. *The Design and Analysis of Research Studies.* New York: Cambridge University Press.1992.

Marascuilo, Leonard A., and Ronald C. Serlin. *Statistical Methods for the Social and Behavioral Sciences.* New York: W.H. Freeman, 1988.

Marsden P.V., and Campbell K.E. 2012. "Reflections on Conceptualizing and Measuring Tie Strength". *Social Forces.* 91, no. 1: 17-23.

Mathematical Social Science Board's Advanced Research Symposium on Social Networks, Paul W. Holland, and Samuel Leinhardt. *Perspectives on Social Network Research.* New York: Academic Press, 1979.

Matland, Richard E. (1995) "Synthesizing the Implementation Literature: The Ambiguity-Conflict Model of Policy Implementation." Journal of Public Administration Research and Theory: J-PART, 5, no. 2. 145-174.

May, Carl. *Towards a General Theory of Implementation.* BioMed Central Ltd. BioMed

Central Ltd, 2013. <http://www.implementationscience.com/content/8/1/18>.

Mazmanian, Daniel A., and Paul A. Sabatier. *Implementation and Public Policy.* Glenview, Ill: Scott, Foresman, 1983.

McDonald, Olivia M. *Acknowledging God in the Decisions of State: A Treatise on Biblically-Informed Statesmanship.* 2nd Ed. Suffolk, VA: Grace House Publishing, 2015.

McDonald, Olivia M. *Formulating a Well-Reasoned Response*, A Limited Access Document, 2010.

McDonald, Olivia M. *Analytical Bridge to the Literary Mind*, A Limited Access Document, 2008.

McKenny A.F.., Short J.C., and Payne G.T. 2013. "Using Computer-Aided Text Analysis to Elevate Constructs: An Illustration Using Psychological Capital". *Organizational Research Methods.* 16, no. 1: 152-184.

Mercado Rami□ rez, Ernesto. *Te□ cnicas para la toma de decisiones: la accio□ n mas importante de la activida humana*. Me□ xico: Limusa, 1991.

Miller, R. L. 2016. "On Messes, Systems Thinking, and Evaluation: A Response to Patton". *American Journal of Evaluation.* 37, no. 2: 266-269.

Mohr, Lawrence B. *Impact Analysis for Program Evaluation.* Thousand Oaks, Calif: Sage Publications, 1995.

Molina, Jose Luis. 2001. "The Informal Organizational Chart in Organizations: An Approach from the Social Network Analysis." *Connections*, 24(1): 78-91.

Müller-Prothmann, Tobias. *Leveraging Knowledge Communication for Innovation Framework, Methods, and Applications of Social Network Analysis in Research and Development.* Frankfurt am Main: Peter Lang, 2006. <http://public.eblib.com/choice/publicfullrecord.aspx?p=1056265>.

National Research Council (U.S.). *Using Science As Evidence in Public Policy*. 2011.

<http://search.ebscohost.com/login.aspx?direct=true&scope=site&db=nlebk&db=nlabk&AN=867617>.

Nelson, Reed E. and K. Michael Mathews, "Cause Maps and Social Network Analysis in Organizational Diagnosis," *Journal of Applied Behavioral Science.* September 1991 vol. 27 no. 3 379-397.

O'Toole, L. J.1997. "The Implications of Democracy in a Networked Bureaucratic World." *Journal of Public Administration Research and Theory,* 7(3), 443-459.

O'toole, Laurence J. 2004. "The Theory-Practice Issue in Policy Implementation Research". *Public Administration.* 82, no. 2: 309-329.

Palisano RJ. 2006. "A Collaborative Model of Service Delivery for Children with Movement Disorders: a Framework for Evidence-Based Decision Making". *Physical Therapy.* 86, no. 9: 1295-305.

Parnell, Gregory S., Parnell, Terry Bresnick, MBA., and S. Tani. *Handbook of Decision Analysis.* John Wiley & Sons, 2013.

Pearson, Michael and Patrick West. 2003. "Drifting Smoke Rings: Social Network Analysis and Markov Processes in a Longitudinal Study of Friendship Groups and Risk-Taking". *Connections,* 25(2): 59-76.

Pituch, K. A., T. A. Whittaker, and W. Chang. 2016. "Multivariate Models for Normal and Binary Responses in Intervention Studies". *American Journal of Evaluation.* 37, no. 2: 270-286.

Prewitt K., and Hauser R. 2013. "Applying the Social and Behavioral Sciences to Policy and Practice". *Issues in Science and Technology.* 29, no. 3: 53-57.

Przeworski, Adam, and Henry Teune. *The Logic of Comparative Social Inquiry.* New York: Wiley-Interscience, 1970.

Real T., Alejandra and Nicolas D. Hasanagas. 2005. "Complete Network Analysis in Research of Organized Interests and Policy Analysis: Indicators, Methodical Aspects and Challenges." *Connections,* 26(20: 89-106.

Renger, Ralph, and Allison Titcomb. 2003. "A Three-Step Approach to Teaching

Logic Models". *American Journal of Evaluation.* 23, no. 4: 493-503.

Rist, Ray C. (1989), "Management Accountability: The Signals Sent by Auditing and Evaluation", *Journal of Public Policy*, 9 (3), July/September, 355-69.

Rivers, Louie. 2006. "A Post-Katrina Call to Action for the Risk Analysis Community." Risk Analysis, 26(1), February, 1-2.

Rogers, Patricia J. 2000. "Causal Models in Program Theory Evaluation". *New Directions for Evaluation.* 2000, no. 87: 47-55.

Rogers, Patricia J. *Program Theory in Evaluation: Challenges and Opportunities.* San Francisco, Calif: Jossey-Bass, 2000.

Rosen, Kenneth H. *Discrete Mathematics and Its Applications.* Boston: McGraw-Hill Higher Education, 2007.

Saaty, Thomas L. and Luis G. Vargas. Decision *Making in Economic, Politic, Social and Technological Environments with the Analytic Hierarchy Process.* Pittsburgh: RWS Publications.1994.

Sabatier, Paul A. *Theories of the Policy Process.* Boulder, Colorado: Westview Press, 2007.

Schoen MW, S Moreland-Russell, K Prewitt, and BJ Carothers. 2014. "Social Network Analysis of Public Health Programs to Measure Partnership". *Social Science & Medicine (1982).* 123: 90-5.

Scholz, Roland W., and Olaf Tietje. *Embedded Case Study Methods: Integrating Quantitative and Qualitative Knowledge.* Thousand Oaks, Calif: Sage Publications, 2002.

Scriven, Michael. *Evaluation Thesaurus.* Newbury Park, Calif: Sage Publications, 1991.

Scriven, Michael. *Reasoning.* New York: McGraw-Hill, 1976.

Shamblin, James E. and G.T.Stevens, Jr. *Operations Research: A Fundamental Approach.* New York: McGraw-Hill Book Company. 1974.

Smith, Stephen L. J. *Tourism Analysis: A Handbook*. Harlow, Essex, England: Longman Scientific & Technical, 1989.

Slottje, Daniel Jonathan. *Measuring the Quality of Life Across Countries: A Multidimensional Analysis*. Boulder: Westview Press, 1991.

Stinchcombe, Arthur L. *Constructing Social Theories*. Chicago: University of Chicago Press. 1987.

Stinchcombe, Arthur L. *When Formality Works: Authority and Abstraction in Law and Organization*. Chicago: University of Chicago Press. 2001.

Stringer, L.C., L. Fleskens, M.S. Reed, J. deVente, and M. Zengin, 2014. "Participatory Evaluation of Monitoring and Modeling of Sustainable Land Management Technologies in Areas Prone to Land Degradation." *Environmental Management* 54:1022-1042. DOA10.1007/s00267-013-0126-5.

Sturges, K. M., and C. Howley. 2016. "Responsive Meta-Evaluation: A Participatory Approach to Enhancing Evaluation Quality". *American Journal of Evaluation.*

United States Department of Homeland Security.2005. *Interim National Preparedness Goal: Homeland Security Presidential Directive 8: National Preparedness.* March 31, 2005.

United States Department of Homeland Security. 2006. The Federal Response to Hurricane Katrina: Lessons Learned. February 24.

United States Government Accountability Office. 2006.Hurricane Katrina: Comprehensive *Policies and Procedures Are Needed to Ensure Appropriate Use of and Accountability for International Assistance*. GAO-06-460.

United States Government Accountability Office. 2006. *GAO-06-365*R *Preliminary Observations on Hurricane Response.*

Varda, Danielle M., and Jessica H. Retrum. 2015. "Collaborative Performance As a Function of Network Members' Perceptions of Success". *Public Performance & Management Review*. 38, no. 4: 632-653.

Vincke, Philippe. 1992. *Multi-Criteria Decision-Aid.* New York: John Wiley & Sons.

Vose, David. *Risk analysis: a quantitative guide*. Chichester [u.a.]: Wiley, 2010.

Wasserman, Stanley and Joseph Galaskiewicz .(eds.) 1994. *Advances in Social Network Analysis.* Thousand Oaks: Sage Publications.

Wenger, Etienne, and William Snyder. *Communities of Practice: The Organizational Frontier.* [Cambridge, Mass.?]: [Harvard Business School Pub.?], 2000.

Wolfe, Alvin W. 2005."Connecting the Dots without Forgetting the Circles." *Connections*, 26(2): 107-119.

Woodland, Rebecca H., and Michael S. Hutton. 2012. "Evaluating Organizational Collaborations: Suggested Entry Points and Strategies". *American Journal of Evaluation.* 33, no. 3: 366-383.

Woodward, M. *Epidemiology: Study Design and Data Analysis.* Boca Raton: Chapman & Hall/CRC, 2005.

Yin, Robert K. *Applications of Case Study Research.* Thousand Oaks: Sage Publications. 2003.

Yin, Robert K. *Case Study Research: Design and Methods.* Thousand Oaks: Sage Publications. 2003.

Zeckhauser, Richard, Ralph L. Keeney, and James K. Sebenius. *Wise Choices : Decisions, Games, and Negotiations.* Boston: Harvard Buiness School Press, 1996.

Zhang, Qiantao, Niall G. MacKenzie, Dylan Jones-Evans, and Robert Huggins. 2016. "Leveraging Knowledge As a Competitive Asset? The Intensity, Performance and Structure of Universities' Entrepreneurial Knowledge Exchange Activities at a Regional Level". *Small Business Economics.* no.

ABOUT THE AUTHOR

Dr. Olivia M. Hidalgo-Hardeman McDonald has over 30 years of combined management and instructional experience in comparative public policy and public management with a proven record of successful instruction in academia. She received her Ph.D. (1980) in political science specializing in public policy, comparative politics, comparative public administration, and quantitative analysis from Purdue University; and, her M.P.A. and B.A. (1978 and 1977) in public affairs, political science, and philosophy from Indiana University. Prior to Liberty University, Dr. McDonald served as "Interim Strategic Communication Lead for the Western Hemisphere" for the Center for Hemispheric Defense Studies, National Defense University, Fort McNair, Virginia. Dr. McDonald's past appointments also include Clinical Professor of Applied Public Policy and Analytical Methods for the Graduate School of Public and International Affairs, University of Pittsburgh; Associate Professor of Public Policy and Quantitative Analysis, member of doctoral faculty serving as Professor of Communication Research at Regent University; Senior Public Policy Research Fellow for Joint Forces Staff College, National Defense University; and, University of Pittsburgh's University Center for International Studies (UCIS) as Associate for the Center for Latin American Studies (CLAS). Dr. McDonald is a co-author of the text, *Public Administration for the Twenty-First Century* published by Harcourt, Brace, and Jovanovich, 1998, as Olivia Hidalgo-Hardeman. Dr. McDonald is also author of *Acknowledging God in the Decisions of State*, 2nd Edition, the book for Christian statesmen.
